THINGS TO DO IN CHILDREN'S WORSHIP

*Bible-based worship material for
Junior Churches and Sunday Schools*

Susan Sayers

Kevin
Mayhew

First published in 1995 by
KEVIN MAYHEW LTD
Buxhall
Stowmarket
Suffolk IP14 3DJ

Things to Do in Children's Worship is extracted
from *Springboard To Worship*.

ISBN 0 86209 649 9
Catalogue No 1500027

1 2 3 4 5 6 7 8 9

Most of the songs in this book can be found in
Come and Praise (BBC Books),
Hymns Old and New (Kevin Mayhew),
Wake up, World! (Kevin Mayhew),
Wonderful World (Kevin Mayhew) and
Songs and Hymns of Fellowship (Kingsway Music).

Editor: Michael Forster
Cover by Claire James
Typesetting and Page Creation by Vicky Brown
Printed and bound in Great Britain.

Foreword

Things to Do in Children's Worship offers a wide range of ideas to help those involved with children's groups in church. In each unit, Bible readings, activities and songs to sing are suggested which can be used together to create an act of worship that is relevant and meaningful for children aged from four to nine.

The material has been arranged thematically in order to allow maximum freedom in adapting it to your own needs. It is not intended as a fully developed 'off the peg' scheme, but as a base on which you can build your own ideas and construct a teaching programme suited to your particular church. The indexes of themes, biblical characters and Bible references will prove invaluable in selecting the units you wish to use.

It is a good idea to keep a record of what you do and save samples in a resource bank. This will be a great help with future planning and preparation. You are free to photocopy what you need, as long as the copies are to be used for the children's work in your church.

Contents

God our Creator and Redeemer 7
God Made the Earth 7
Wonderful World! 8
God Saves his People 9
Jesus the Bread of Life 10
Children of God 11
Jesus Suffered for Us 12
One Great Family 13

God With Us 14
Look Out For God 14
God Saves and Judges 15
God Forgives and Heals 16
Get Ready for God 17
Good News for Mary 18
Jesus is Coming 19
Prepare the Way! 20
The Bible Shows us Jesus 21
Jesus is Born 22
The Prophets Point to Jesus 23
The Light of the World 24
Who is Jesus? 25

The Ministry of Jesus 26
I Can See! 26
Individuals Matter to God 27
Room For Us All! 28
The Good Shepherd 29
Sharing Jesus' Baptism 30
The King on a Donkey 31
How Faith Grows 32
The Light of God's Glory 33
Let the Light Shine 34

New Life in Christ 35
Saved by Christ 35
Sign of God's Glory 36
God Offers Us New Life 37
Children of God and Friends of Jesus 38
Churches, Temples and People 39
Jesus is Alive! 40

Faith, Trust and Hope 41

Courage and Commitment 41
Faith and Works 42
Abraham's Faith 43
Faith and Prayer 44
God's Mysterious Spirit 45
Faith Without Seeing 46
God Turns Sorrow into Joy 47
God's Way is Different – and Better! 48
Healing and Wholeness 49
Hope and Pray 50
Our God reigns 51
The Hope of Heaven 52
Stand Firm 53
Living by Faith 54
God Changes Lives 55
Keeping Hope Alive 56

Temptation, Sin, Forgiveness 57

Loving and Forgiving 57
Ready and Waiting 58
Forgiveness 59
Seventy Times Seven 60
The Cost of Love and Forgiveness 61
Jesus Wipes Away Sins 62
Honest Worship 63
Listen to God! 64
Taking Responsibility 65
Falling Away from Goodness 66

Worship, Discipleship, Mission 67

Good Neighbours 67
Love in Action 68
Choosing God's Way 69
God of Surprises 70
Hear God Calling 71
God is Shown to the World 72
Offering and Sharing 73
Good will Overcome Evil 74
New Beginnings with God 75
The Way, the Truth and the Life 76
God Makes Friends 77
Being the People of God 78
Be Like Jesus 79
Our Mission to All People 80

The Cost of Christian Living   81
Life-giving Spirit   82
Doing the Right Thing   83
Salt and Light   84
Generous Giving   85
Loving Service   86
The Best Offering   87
Using God's Gifts   88
God's Law of Love   89

Index of Uses

90

God Made the Earth

Things to Read

Genesis 1:1-31a
John 1:1-14

A children's version of this creation story is available called *God Makes the World* (Kevin Mayhew).

Things to Do

Read the children the story of creation, either from the Bible, or from a good Bible story book. In prayer together thank God for the wonderful world he has made for us. Then give out lumps of modelling clay and make some models of some of God's plants and creatures. Arrange everything on a large tray which has been covered with green and blue paper to represent the land and sea. Write a title for the display: GOD MADE THE WORLD, and bring it into the church for everyone to see.

Things to Sing

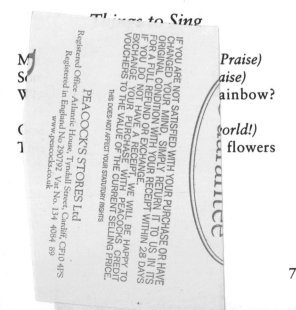

M̲   *Praise)*
S̲   *aise)*
V̲   ainbow?

C̲   *orld!)*
T̲   flowers

Wonderful World!

Things to Read

Genesis 2:4b-9
John 3:1-8
Revelation 4

Things to Do

On tables around the edge of the room put a varied collection of things created by God, together with hands-on activities. Let the children spend some time exploring these.

Display suggestions:

Assorted rocks and pebbles: How many colours can you see?

Sea shells: Put a shell to your ear. What can you hear?

Autumn leaves: Find which trees these came from, with a chart.

A globe: Can you find Britain? The Pacific Ocean? Australia?

Feathers: Look for the hooks on the end of the feathers with a magnifying glass.

Animal pictures or models: Which box does each animal belong to? (With boxes labelled 'Meat eaters', 'Grass eaters')

Prism or cut glass beads: Can you make rainbows?

Containers of sand, dried peas, bird seed, sheep's wool: Feel the different textures.

Magnets and a box of things to test for magnetism: What will the magnet attract?

When everyone has sampled everything, gather in a circle to talk about the amazing world God has made for us to live in and look after. How can we look after it well? Thank God together for all he has made, and help the children write down their thanks to God for the things they find most amazing, beautiful, powerful or clever. Cut round the decorated prayers, stick double-sided sticky tape on the back and bring them into church.

Things to Sing

If I were a butterfly *(Hymns Old and New)*
Morning has broken *(Come and Praise)*
Somebody greater *(Come and Praise)*
God made the earth *(Wake up, World!)*
God is making a wonderful world *(Wake up, World!)*

8

God Saves his People

Things to Read

Exodus 6:2-8
Mark 13:5-13

Things to Do

Remind the children about Abraham, who was called by God to leave his home city and travel to the Promised Land. Explain how, many generations later, the people of Israel settled in Egypt during a long drought; how the Egyptians later began using them as slaves and treating them badly.

(This should be very brief, but it is important for the children to begin to see the 'shape' of God's plan for salvation, rather than a number of unconnected events.)

Show the children a picture of Moses as a baby, hidden in his basket. This was to be the person God had chosen to lead his people to freedom. When he grew up God told him that he had heard his people's groaning and crying, and was going to help them and set them free. (With older children read the Exodus passage here.) Moses trusted God, and God kept his promise.

Food in the Desert (The Palm Tree Bible) emphasises the growth of faith through the hardships in the wilderness. Read this to the children, showing them all the pictures, to give them an idea of how God can be trusted, and how he kept his promise to Moses and his people.

Have ready the separate letters of GOD CAN BE TRUSTED on sheets of thin card, and a length of string. Give the letters out for the children to decorate and cut out, punch two holes in the top of each letter, and string them up in the right order so that the unjumbled message appears. If possible, let the children bring this into church and hang it up between two chairs, so that everyone can see.

Things to Sing

Moses, I know you're the man *(Hymns Old and New)*
Lead my people to freedom! *(Wake up, World!)*
Keep on travelling on! *(Wake up, World!)*

Jesus the Bread of Life

Things to Read

John 6:5-14,35

A children's version, *The Biggest Picnic in History*, can be found in *A Story a Hug and a Prayer*, and a dramatised version in *Wonderful World!* (Kevin Mayhew).

Things to Sing

Feed the hungry people *(Wake up, World)*

Break the bread and pour the wine *(Wake up, World)*

Things to Do

Talk with the children about what they have eaten for breakfast. Then say something like: 'Well, you won't be needing any more food today, then, will you.' Pretend to be surprised that they are expecting to have more food later on. Why? Because they will get hungry again.

Now show the children a picture of Jesus feeding the 5,000 with bread and fish. Everyone had enough to eat at the time. But would they get hungry again? Yes; one loaf will not keep us alive for ever. Jesus told the people that he was like a loaf of bread – not to keep our bodies alive but to feed the spirit part of us which can live for ever. If we have Jesus living in us we shall never be spiritually hungry again; he will keep us full of love, peace and joy.

Whenever we eat bread we can remember that we need Jesus, our bread of life, as well. Help the children make this bread basket to use at home, and pop a roll into each to eat with their lunch.

Children of God

Things to Read

Isaiah 7:10-14
John 1:14-18
Galatians 4:1-7

Things to Do

Discuss with the children what it means to be adopted. Some may have personal experience of being 'chosen' in this way into a family. They may have come across 'Cabbage Patch' dolls which come with an adoption certificate. There are often advertisements in local newspapers about children in care who are hoping to find a family willing to adopt them.

It is important that even young children have the opportunity to talk about such matters in a caring, sensitive atmosphere, and they are often touchingly aware of the importance of belonging to a family unit.

Now give the children lumps of modelling clay and ask them to make some kind of person-creature that they would like as a friend if it were alive. When the creatures are finished, display them and enjoy them.

Wouldn't it be wonderful if we really could bring them to life! Explain how God created beings whom he loved and actually brought to life, and see if they can guess the names of some of them. And not only did he give us life, he adopted us; so that makes us very, very special – we must be children in God's family. He is our parent who loves us enough to want us to eat, sleep, play, work, sing, laugh and cry in his company.

Write this notice to put with the models and bring the whole thing into church.

God made us, gave us life,
and chose us as his children

God made us, gave us life,
and chose us as his children

Things to Sing

God knows me *(Come and Praise)*
I'm black, I'm white, I'm short, I'm tall *(Wake up, World!)*
Break the bread and pour the wine *(Wake up, World!)*

Jesus Suffered for Us

Things to Read

Isaiah 50:4-9a
John 16:1-11

Things to Do

Jesus was not just a good man but actually the Son of God. Draw a large cross as the sign of Jesus, in the centre of a sheet of paper. The prophets in the Old Testament spoke about what Jesus would be like and what he would do. Now draw in (or stick on) some people on the left side of the cross, looking towards it. Write in some speech balloons with quotations referring to the Christ:

Daniel 7:13-14
I saw . . . there came one like a son of man . . . and to him was given dominion and glory and kingdom.

Micah 5:2
From you, Bethlehem, shall come a ruler . . . who shall feed his flock in the strength of the Lord.

Isaiah 60:3
Kings shall come to the brightness of your rising.

Isaiah 53:5
He was wounded for our wrongdoing.

Then discuss with the children how these fit in with Jesus' life. They will see that his suffering for us is mentioned; the cross is part of the loving.

Jesus told his friends that if they wanted to follow him they would have to be prepared to suffer as well. Ask the children to colour and cut out pictures of themselves to stick on the right side of the cross, looking towards it.

Things to Sing

The Servant King
He was born in the winter *(Wake up, World!)*
Do this when you remember me *(Wake up, World!)*

One Great Family

Things to Read

Mark 10:2-16
Ephesians 5:25-6:4

Things to Do

Bring along a selection of toy farmyard and zoo animals and people and let the children group them into families of mother, father and baby. Or you could use a Happy Families set of cards to sort into families.

Now read the children the story of creation; the *Palm Tree Bible* series has a version called *God makes the world*. They will see how God started the family idea right at the beginning of humanity's creation. Show them some wedding pictures and point out that it is God who joins the couple in marriage.

Using card tubes, scraps of net and other material, colour pens and glue, help them make a bride and bridegroom holding hands.

Things to Sing

He's got the whole world in his hand
I'm black, I'm white, I'm short, I'm tall
(Wake up, World!)
Break the bread and pour the wine *(Wake up, World!)*
Out to the great wide world we go *(Wake up, World!)*

GOD WITH US

Look Out for God

Things to Read

Isaiah 33:17-22
Matthew 25:1-13

Things to Do

Tell the children today's gospel story, making it clear that it is a story Jesus told, not a real event. To help in the telling, have two strips of card, each with five bridesmaids on it.

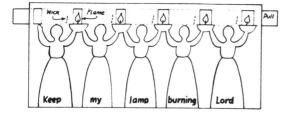

Five have extra oil in a flask, five do not. At the point where the lamps go out, pull the strip along, so that the wicks show instead of the flames.

When they have heard the story and what it tells us about keeping ourselves ready for Jesus, the children can make their own strip of bridesmaids with flames that go out. Write on each: 'Keep my lamp burning Lord' with one word on each bridesmaid.

Things to Sing

Come on and celebrate *(Songs and Hymns of Fellowship)*
In the winter nights are dark *(Wake up, World!)*
Kum ba yah

God Saves and Judges

Things to Read

Isaiah 51:4-11
Matthew 25:31-46
Romans 13:8-end

Things to Do

Tell the children that we are getting ourselves ready for the coming of Jesus, not just as a baby at Christmas time but also the time when he will come again in great glory. We know this will happen because Jesus told us about it, but we don't know when, so we need to be prepared all the time.

With the aid of pictures and/or items of uniform, talk about people who always have to keep themselves ready because they don't know when their help will be needed —such as firemen, police, emergency staff at a hospital, lifeboatmen etc. How do they make sure they are ready?
– by practising rescues,
– by keeping themselves fit,
– by keeping their equipment well-oiled and repaired.

Now read the gospel story, asking the children to listen out for ways we can get ourselves ready for Jesus' coming. Have the different examples ('When I was hungry, you gave me food' etc) already written out on pieces of card, so that when they are mentioned after the reading you can display them.

Produce an empty carton and place all the cards inside, explaining that all these things are part of LOVING. (Write this in large letters on the carton.) Have some other pieces of card available and help the children write and decorate other practical ways of showing a caring love to others, such as offering to help Mum and Dad, sharing toys with others, being friendly to a child at school who is often lonely, or being pleased at someone else's success.

Carry the carton up to the altar at the offertory, and let the children process to the altar and put their card into the box. If there is time, these could be read out for the congregation to hear. They are offered along with the collection.

Things to Sing

Love is something if you give it away
You shall go out with joy (Songs and Hymns of Fellowship)
In the winter nights are dark (Wake up, World!)
I'm black, I'm white, I'm short, I'm tall (Wake up, World!)
Out to the great wide world we go (Wake up, World!)

God Forgives and Heals

Things to Read

Zephaniah 3:14-end
Mark 2:1-12

A children's version, both as a story and as a drama, *The Man Who Came in Through the Roof,* can be found in *Wonderful World!* (Kevin Mayhew).

Things to Do

Tell today's story of the paralytic who was let down through the roof, using a simple model which the children make first. One group makes a house from a white shoe box. At this stage do not mention the way the man's friend got him to Jesus; just talk about the typical design of such a house with outside steps to a flat roof in which there was often an opening.

Other children make a stretcher-bed with a paralysed man on it, and others make a large crowd of people. Arrange the model on sand-coloured paper and put a few model donkeys and chickens around, and a palm tree or two.

Place Jesus and his friends in the house first, and add other visitors as you explain how word got around that Jesus could heal the sick. When the men arrive with their paralysed friend the children will see that they can't get to Jesus. Ask what they might do now. Give up? Seeing the problem will help them appreciate the men's faith and their determination and persistence. They may even suggest using the hole in the roof.

All through the story help them to identify with the different characters so that they can, in some sense, become 'eye witnesses' to the events.

Things to Sing

God knows me *(Come and Praise)*
Jesus had all kinds of friends *(Wake up, World!)*
God is making a wonderful world *(Wake up, World!)*
Out to the great wide world we go! *(Wake up, World!)*

Get Ready for God

Things to Read

Isaiah 52:7-10
1 Thessalonians 5:1-11
Luke 21:25-33

Things to Do

Bring in an alarm clock with a really loud ring or buzz. First talk to the children about how lovely it is when you're all warm and asleep in bed in the morning and then suddenly: BRRRRRRR! shatters your peace. Talk about how alarm clocks jerk you awake so you can get ready and not miss the day's activities. Tell them that as well as coming as a baby at Christmas time, 2000 years ago, Jesus will come again one day with glory and power. We don't know when it will be, so we must be ready for him.

Now read the first paragraph of the suggested gospel story. You may feel the Good News translation is better suited to children's understanding – it is worth reading a few different versions to choose one most suitable for your particular group.
How can we get ready for Jesus?
Have written on a chart or blackboard:
1. Find out more about him – reading and praying.
2. Try to live the Jesus way – being loving and kind.

If you do not have a church library for children, this might be a good time to start one. Try to encourage the children to get into the habit of reading. Perhaps families might read the books together. Give each child a card on which they can record the titles of books about Jesus which they have read, and on the back print this prayer which the children can decorate.

Things to Sing

You can't stop rain from falling down *(Hymns Old and New)*
In the winter, nights are dark *(Wake up, World!)*
Out to the great wide world we go! *(Wake up, World!)*

Good News for Mary

Things to Read

Isaiah 11:1-9
1 Corinthians 1:26-end
Luke 1:26-38a

Things to Do

Beforehand, prepare a picture of some houses in a street drawn on thin card, and cut round the doors so that they open and close. Also make a simple wooden-spoon or mop puppet.

First talk with the children about any good news they would like to share, and choose someone to knock on the door of each house to tell their news.

At the first house let the puppet say: 'Go away – I'm busy!', at the second house: 'Pardon? . . . pardon? . . . I can't hear a word!'; at the third house: 'You don't expect me to believe THAT, do you?'; and at the fourth house: 'Hallo! Nice to see you . . . oh really? How lovely!' Discuss with them the different ways of receiving news, and how we need to welcome Jesus when he speaks to us, instead of being deaf, or too busy, or not believing what he says.

Now show the children a picture of God's messenger bringing some very important news to Mary. Who was the messenger? What was his news? Think back to the ways people sometimes react – did Mary say she was too busy, or couldn't hear, or didn't believe the angel? Read together the way Mary listened carefully and said she would certainly let God's will be done in her.

Things to Sing

Kum ba yah
In the winter, nights are dark *(Wake up, World!)*
Out to the great wide world we go! *(Wake up, World!)*

Jesus is Coming

Things to Read

Matthew 1:18-23
Revelation 21:1-7

Things to Do

Talk about how we prepare for Christmas, and remind them of what we are all getting ready to celebrate – Jesus' birthday. Tell the children about how Mary and Joseph would be getting ready: packing food and clothing for their journey to Bethlehem, loading up their donkey, bringing baby clothes in case the baby arrives while they are away from home etc. Have some bags of nuts and raisins, dry biscuits, brightly coloured rugs, baby clothes and swaddling (length of sheeting). Put these out on the table as you discuss the things Mary and Joseph needed, and let the children pack them into cloth bags.

Now help them to make a small crib to put up in their homes, with a candle to light. Below is a pop-up version to try. The children will need scissors, glue and colouring pencils. Perhaps the finished crib could be offered at the altar before being taken home.

Things to Sing

Out to the great wide world we go! *(Wake up, World!)*

In the winter, nights are dark *(Wake up, World!)*

One more step along the world I go *(Come and Praise)*

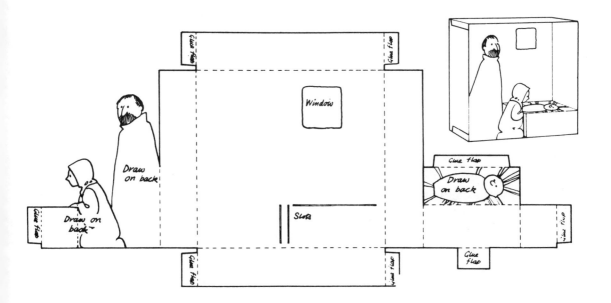

Prepare the Way!

Things to Read

Isaiah 40:1-11
John 1:19-28

Things to Do

First talk with the children about how their town or country prepares its streets for important visitors such as royalty, a winning football team or a film star. There may be flags hung up, streamers waving, a red carpet rolled out on the pavement and flowers planted round all the lamp posts for instance. If you have any photographs of such events, or a local carnival, show them around.

Now read them Isaiah 40:3-5 and the first part of today's gospel reading, where John the Baptist uses the prophecy to explain his own job. Unroll a length of white material, about a yard wide and four yards long. (A double sheet split down the middle and joined end to end makes the right size: it is important that it looks big.)

The children are going to turn this strip of boring material into a highway for Jesus. At Christmas time it can be laid down in church so that when the Christ child is brought to the manger he is carried along the children's highway.

Have ready plenty of colourful oddments of material, a really efficient fabric glue, scissors, pens and templates. Discuss ways in which we can prepare ourselves for Jesus, and write these at intervals along the highway with coloured pens. On flower shapes they can write thank you messages.

Things to Sing

One more step along the world I go *(Come and Praise)*
Out to the great wide world we go *(Wake up, World!)*
Pick up your feet and go *(Wake up, World!)*

The Bible Shows us Jesus

Things to Read

Isaiah 55:1-11
John 5:36b-end
2 Timothy 3:14-4:5

Things to Do

Set up a treasure hunt with clues which direct the children from one place to another.

The 'treasure' is a torch or bicycle lamp. Switch it on and talk with the children about how useful it is in helping us find our way in the dark, without tripping over things or causing accidents.

Now show them several different Bibles, explaining that in the Bible there are lots of clues to direct us to find the light of the world – Jesus. Give out these clues to different children and help them find the places which lead us to Jesus. You could have these already written up on a sheet of paper, each text covered with a question mark until the child finds the reference in the Bible: Listen to John the Baptist (Mark 1:7); Hear what God said (Mark 1:11); Where does the Spirit settle? (Mark 1:10).

Tell the children that there are lots of other clues every day which can lead us to Jesus, such as the beautiful and amazing things in nature, kind or unselfish behaviour; Bible stories and stories of the saints, help given when we need it, songs and poems etc.

Give the children this duplicated paper with a picture of Jesus in the centre which they can colour in. Then each day of the week they fill in one circle either with words or a drawing, with something that has directed them to think of Jesus and know him better. Ask them to bring these back next week.

Things to Sing

Come on and celebrate *(Songs and Hymns of Fellowship)*
Kum ba yah
I'm black, I'm white, I'm short, I'm tall *(Wake up, World!)*
In the winter, nights are dark *(Wake up, World!)*

21

Jesus is Born

Things to Read

Isaiah 9:2,6-7
Luke 2:1-7
Luke 2:8-20

Children's versions of both these gospel stories, both as stories and as dramas, can be found in *Wonderful World!* (Kevin Mayhew) entitled *No Room* and *Never Mind the Sheep, Look for the Baby.*

Things to Do

Many churches find the Christingle symbolism helpful; leaflets providing an outline of Christingle, using the traditional orange (as the world) and candle (as the light of Christ) can be obtained from The Children's Society, Old Town Hall, Kennington Road, London SEll 4QD.

It is important that children feel part of the family worship at the festival. Perhaps they could have practised a special carol which they can sing during the service, or they may present a nativity play or tableau during or just after the gospel reading.

Elderly residents in nursing homes love to hear children singing, too. If cards are made and distributed at the same time, the children will be providing a most valuable ministry.

Things to Sing

Jesus Christ is here *(Come and Praise)*
Born in a stable *(Wake up, World!)*
Or choose from many traditional Christmas Carols

The Prophets Point to Jesus

Things to Read

Isaiah 64:1-7
Luke 4:14-21
Romans 15:4-13

Things to Do

So as to get across the idea of fulfilled prophecy, make a 'scroll' by rolling a sheet of paper stuck on to sticks at either end, with a ribbon or tape on it for fastening. If possible, copy a little Hebrew writing on to it, as well as the prophecy included in today's gospel story, (Isaiah 61:1-2a).

Show it to the children, ask them to guess what it is, and explain how, many years before Jesus was born, some people (prophets) were used by God to be messengers. Through them, God told his people that one day he would send someone very important who would save them and show them the right way to live. What they said was written down on scrolls like this one.

Ask one of the older children to read the first part of today's gospel story, up to the point when Jesus is handed the scroll. Let one of the younger children hand the reader the home-made scroll. The passage from Isaiah 61:1-2a is read from it. The teacher now tells the last part of the gospel, with the children acting it out.

Recap with them about the kind of things the promised Saviour would do, matching them up bit by bit with what they know of Jesus. Have lots of pictures, Bible story books, and an illustrated Bible available to refer to. The children will be able to see that the prophecy really was coming true in Jesus.

Help the children make their own scrolls, with the prophecy stuck on. Garden canes, cut to size, make inexpensive sticks, and the paper is best attached with strong glue.

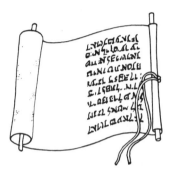

Things to Sing

Morning has broken
Come on and celebrate (Songs and Hymns of Fellowship)
I'm black, I'm white, I'm short, I'm tall (Wake up, World!)

The Light of the World

Things to Read

Isaiah 60:1-6
Matthew 2:1-12, 19-23

A children's version of the 'Wise Men' story, in both story and drama form, *Ride that Camel! Follow that Star!* can be found in *Wonderful World!* (Kevin Mayhew).

Things to Do

Prepare a cereal box 'television' and a strip of paper showing the night sky, the wise men on their journey, their visit to Herod, their adoration of Jesus and their departure by another route. Use the drawings below as a guideline, or cut out pictures from Christmas cards and stick them on.

Tell the children the story of the wise men, rolling the pictures along as you do so; or ask two children to do the spoon twisting.

Talk about how we can all be like the star by shining brightly to lead people to Jesus. With their help, make a list of practical ways we can do this:

- stay close to Jesus
- get to know the Bible
- be kind and loving
- stand up for what is right
- let others know you're a Christian
- enjoy and care for God's world

Have six strips of card about 1 metre long and 5 cms wide and lay them down on the floor to make a star shape like this:

Write one of the six guidelines for being a star on each strip of card and let the children decorate them with tinsel and glue. Staple the strips together and carry the star into church, placing it where it may be clearly seen.

Things to Sing

Pick up your feet and go *(Wake up! World!)*
Wise men from a country far *(Wonderful World!)*
In the winter, nights are dark *(Wake up, World!)*

Who is Jesus?

Things to Read

Malachi 3:1-5
Matthew 11:2-15

Things to Do

Have ready a display of some of the lovely things in our world which enrich our lives and make us thankful. These may include water and food, pictures of the seasons and nature, warmth and light (candles) and photographs of people. Begin with thanks and praise for the God who loves us and gives us so much.

Then, using pictures from an illustrated Bible, tell the children about John the Baptist, sent by God to help people get ready for the Lord's coming. Many listened to what he said and made a big effort to change into more caring, honest and thankful people. As a sign that they were washed clean from evil, John waded into the river Jordan with them and prayed over them while they were dipped in the clean water. This was called Baptism. Remind the children that among those John baptised was Jesus himself. John recognised Jesus as being the Lord.

But then Herod had John arrested and thrown into prison, where he was chained up all on his own. He heard stories about what Jesus was doing and was surprised. He had expected the Lord to unite everyone in a great body that would drive out the Romans so the country would once more be free. Instead, Jesus was talking about loving our enemies, caring for one another – even people from other nations and races

– and he seemed to be making friends with bad people as well as good. Could this Jesus really be the Lord?

Poor John must have felt anxious, miserable and muddled. So he sent some of his own followers to Jesus to ask him straight out: 'Are you the one who is to come, or are we to expect some other?'

Jesus understood John's doubts. He thought of the best way to put John's mind at rest. He knew that John had read the prophets' writings again and again and knew them inside out. So he quoted to John's messengers the prophecy about the blind receiving their sight, the lame walking and the lepers being made clean. The messengers could see that Jesus was making all this come true! John would understand that Jesus' kingdom was to come about by loving rather than fighting, however good the cause.

Help the children make up figures for a flannelgraph, by colouring, cutting out and mounting on felt. Then, with the children putting the figures on to the flannelgraph, go through the main points of today's teaching.

Things to Sing

Come on and celebrate (Songs and Hymns of Fellowship)
He was born in the winter (Wake up, World!)
Out to the great wide world we go (Wake up, World!)
Jesus had all kinds of friends (Wake up, World!)

THE MINISTRY OF JESUS

I Can See!

Things to Read

Mark 10:46-end
Ephesians 4:17-end

Things to Do

Talk with the children about how difficult it is for blind people to go shopping, cook or even walk along pavements where bikes have been left around. Ask them to shut their eyes for a minute while they try to do an ordinary task like laying a table or putting their shoes and socks on.

Explain how sometimes we can all be 'blind' to other people's needs or to how we are making life difficult for someone. Jesus wants to give us all our sight back.

Now read or tell them the story in today's gospel passage, getting a few to mime it as you go. Then help them make these masks to make the point of seeing God's way.

Things to Sing

Jesus had all kinds of friends *(Wake up, World!)*
Out to the great wide world we go *(Wake up, World!)*
God made the earth *(Wake up, World!)*

Individuals Matter to God

Things to Read

Isaiah 63:7-14
Acts 8:26-38
Luke 15:1-10

A children's version of the Lost Sheep story, in narrative and drama form, entitled *What a Silly Sheep!* can be found in *Wonderful World!* (Kevin Mayhew).

Things to Do

There are plenty of good versions of these two parables specially for children. Read them one, showing the pictures as you go. Talk about what it feels like to be lost, and then to be found. Remind them that Jesus doesn't want ANY of his 'sheep' to be lost, and we need to learn to love as much as that. Every person is special to God, and that's why we must treat every person as special and precious– even if we don't particularly like the way they behave.

Together make this model to illustrate the story of the lost sheep, with the shepherd out looking for it. They can each make a sheep out of card and cotton wool.

 Cut out and stick cotton wool on card.

Things to Sing

I'm black, I'm white, I'm short, I'm tall *(Wake up, World!)*
God is making a wonderful world *(Wake up, World!)*
Out to the great wide world we go *(Wake up, World!)*

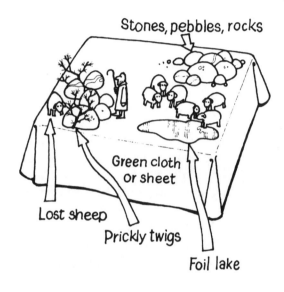

Stones, pebbles, rocks

Green cloth or sheet

Lost sheep

Prickly twigs

Foil lake

Room For Us All!

Things to Read

Isaiah 61:1-7
John 21:1-14
1 Corinthians 15:1-11

Things to Do

Tell or read the story of the disciples fishing and seeing Jesus on the beach.

Divide the group into two. One group prepares the acting out (give lots of help and encourage the shy ones to participate).

The other group cuts out lots of fish, all different colours, shapes and sizes. Have a net (old curtain) and an upturned table as a boat. Then the actors perform to the fish makers.

If this were prepared beforehand, the children could present their performance during the reading. Otherwise, let them take a fish home with them to remind them of what happened. Suggest they tell their families, or draw a picture of it to bring back next week.

Things to Sing

One hundred and fifty-three *(Wake up, World!)*
Jesus had all kinds of friends *(Wake up, World!)*
I'm black, I'm white, I'm short, I'm tall *(Wake up, World!)*

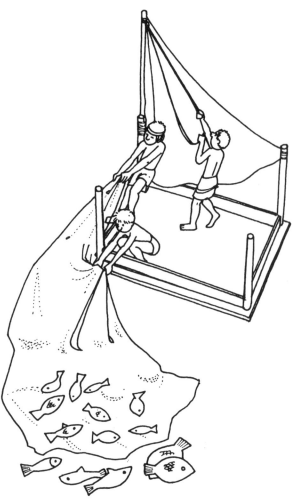

The Good Shepherd

Things to Read

Ezekiel 34:7-16
1 Peter 5:1-11
John 10:7-16

Things to Do

Have a green sheet of paper on the table with some farmyard models of sheep and lambs, a sheepdog and a shepherd. Talk with the children about what a shepherd's job involves. Some of them may have watched sheep being moved from one pasture to another. What would happen to the sheep if there was no shepherd? Talk about the way they stray into danger, and other ways they are vulnerable.

Now build a model of a sheep fold, or pen, which is used in the country Jesus lived in. Make it from small stones or from plasticine which has been given a stone pattern. The shepherd lay in the doorway to sleep, so he was the door! That kept the sheep all safe inside.

Next read the first part of today's Gospel, and help them understand that Jesus is the Good Shepherd and we are the sheep and lambs.

Then help the children to make sheep headgear on which is written: 'The Lord is my Shepherd'. Perhaps they could process, bleating, into church and kneel for a moment of silence in front of the altar before joining their families.

Things to Sing

God knows me (Come and Praise)
Out to the great wide world we go (Wake up, World!)
I'm black, I'm white, I'm short, I'm tall (Wake up, World!)

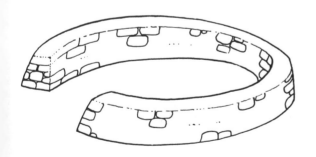

Sharing Jesus' Baptism

Things to Read

Isaiah 42:1-7
Matthew 3:13-end
Ephesians 2:1-10

Things to Do

If you have any pictures of the Jordan, show these first, so that the children realise that it is a real place and can identify more easily with events there.

Also have a large baking tray, some earth or sand, metal foil, stones and twigs, and plasticine. Explain that you are all going to make a model of the Jordan and then let the children help assemble it. With the foil make a trough which can be filled with water for the river. Plasticine models of people can also be made, one of whom is John, and one Jesus. The rest are the crowds. Make a dove too.

Then tell the story of Jesus' baptism, moving the models as you do so. Rattle a sheet of thick card as God's voice speaks.

Give the children cards to fill and colour, like this:

Things to Sing

God knows me *(Come and Praise)*
He was born in the winter in a draughty shed *(Wake up, World!)*
I'm black, I'm white, I'm short, I'm tall *(Wake up, World!)*
Out to the great wide world we go *(Wake up, World!)*
Kum ba yah

The King on a Donkey

Things to Read

Philippians 2:5-11
Matthew 21:1-9

A children's version of this story, in narrative and drama form, entitled *The Donkey's Day Out* can be found in *Wonderful World!* (Kevin Mayhew).

Things to Do

Encourage the children to bring large leaves or branches to wave in the procession, or colourful streamers. They may also join in the crowd sections of the gospel story if they are in the church at this point.

If not, read the story, and then help the children make a model of the scene. Use a large tray as the base, with hills of crumpled paper under a green towel. The track is a strip of brown or beige material. Houses can be made from white paper like this:

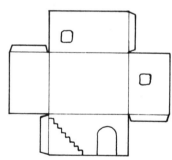

and palm trees from green paper like this:

Have a farmyard model of a donkey and make plasticine figures, waving real leaves. Pieces of material cut out can be laid on the path in front of Jesus.

Display the finished model where the rest of the congregation can see it.

Things to Sing

We have a king who rides a donkey
Out to the great wide world we go *(Wake up, World!)*

How Faith Grows

Things to Read

Proverbs 3:1-8
Luke 8:4b-15

Things to Do

Have some grain (pearl barley will do, if
no wheat is available) and a baking tray
arranged with the varied surfaces on it
like this:

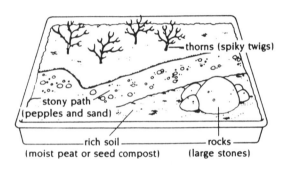

As you tell the story, sprinkle the seed so
that some falls on each section. Talk
about which will not grow and which
will do the best. You could have some
fresh plants to press into the good soil to
emphasise the point.

Now explain how Jesus used this story
to tell us about how people react to
God's good news. See if they can work
out what some of the images mean. Then
help the children to write captions for
each section, stick them on lolly sticks
and push them into the model. Others
can decorate the background and title.

The whole model will then look
something like this:

Bring the model into church and display
it where the rest of the congregation can
see it.

Things to Sing

Think of a world without any flowers
   (*Come and Praise*)
We can plough and dig the land *(Wake
   up, World!)*
Out to the great wide world we go *(Wake
   up, World!)*

The Light of God's Glory

Things to Read

Exodus 3:1-6
Matthew 17:1-13
2 Peter 1:16-19

Things to Sing

Shine, Jesus, shine!
The voice from the bush *(Wake up, World!)*

Things to Do

Have lots of candles, flowers and glass in a beautiful arrangement, with quiet music playing as the children come in.

Point out the way the light and beauty are reflected in the glass. Talk about the lovely things in our world which reflect God's glory in this way – sunny days, rain drops, snowflakes, spring flowers, animals, cobwebs etc.– and thank him for them in a prayer or song.

Then tell them how one day, Jesus showed his glory, the glory of God, not as a reflection but directly. Tell the story of the transfiguration as music plays in the background, explaining that God is full of glory like that all the time, even if we only see it sometimes.

Give each child a card folded like this:

Have the eyes and words already on it. Let them fill the centre with all kinds of lovely things, either drawn, or cut out and stuck on.

Let the Light Shine

Things to Read

Exodus 34:29-end
Luke 9:28-36

A children's version of this story can be found in the *Palm Tree Bible* series, entitled *The Secret on the Mountain*

Things to Sing

Shine, Jesus, shine
In the winter, nights are dark *(Wake up, World)*
Give me oil in my lamp

Things to Do

Tell the story of *the transfiguration*. This works well on tape with music in the background as Jesus is transfigured. Alternatively, have a guitar playing, or taped music while the story is told.

Have the children sitting in a circle round a table with a white candle on it. Have the candle lit as Jesus is transfigured, and blown out when the cloud passes over and only Jesus is left.

Give each child a candle (unlit). Show how one light can light all of these. In the same way, we can all be lit by Jesus.

Give out squares of paper with a candle drawn on and slits above.

Ask children to colour the candle and the flame and wick. Stick into books with a strip of sellotape top and bottom. Above it write: 'The bright love of Jesus can light my life.'

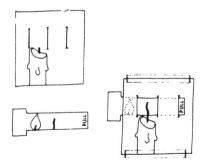

New Life in Christ

Saved by Christ

Things to Read

Luke 8:41-end
Acts 4:8-12

Various children's versions of the gospel story are available. *The Palm Tree Bible* version is called *Becky Gets Better.* Another version, presented both as narrative and as a drama, entitled *Get Up, Little Girl,* is in *Wonderful World!* (Kevin Mayhew).

Things to Do

The children will get a lot from joining in the acting of the gospel story, along with the adults. If you are not planning on acting it in the church, then act it out with the children, perhaps reading or summarising the story for them first.

Have a time, too, to praise and thank God for all his gifts to us, especially the gift of life and the wonderful creation he has given us to enjoy. Pray with the children for those who are ill, blind, deaf or disabled in any way and discuss practical ways the group can help.

Things to Sing

Give me oil in my lamp
Come on and celebrate
You shall go out with joy
Out to the great wide world we go *(Wake up, World!)*
Jesus had all kinds of friends *(Wake up, World!)*

Sign of God's Glory

Things to Read

Exodus 33:12-end
John 2:1-11

A children's version of this story, as narrative and as drama, entitled *A Wedding With No Wine*, can be found in *Wonderful World!* (Kevin Mayhew).

Things to Sing

Jesus turned the water into wine *(Wake up, World!)*
Break the bread and pour the wine *(Wake up, World!)*
Do this when you remember me *(Wake up, World!)*

Things to Do

Display some posters of vineyards – travel agents should be able to supply some pictures – and have a cluster of grapes on the table (seedless are best for young children). Share the grapes out, and talk about how the juice is squeezed out and mellowed carefully in vats before being bottled and drunk, perhaps on a special happy occasion like weddings, or, in some countries, with everyday meals.

Read or tell them about the wedding in Cana when the wine ran out, and Jesus gave them wine from water.

When have they seen wine used in church? Talk about the celebration which we share there – Jesus shares his life with us.

Help the children make a card like this:

God Offers Us New Life

Things to Read

Deuteronomy 6:17-end
John 6:25-35
Romans 6:3-11

Things to Sing

Kum ba yah
One more step along the world I go
(Come and Praise)
Out to the great wide world we go!
(Wake up, World!)

Things to Do

Ask the children to remember some of Jesus' healing works when he was living as a man in Galilee. Explain how he always felt sorry for people who were sad or ill, and wanted to make them well.

Now tell the story of today's gospel reading, referring to a picture if possible.

If the children know of anyone who is ill the whole group can pray for them, imagining Jesus comforting them and asking him to make them well.

Then the children can make this pop-up card. They will need a piece of folded paper, and a semi-circle marked with fold lines; coloured pencils, scissors and glue. Decorate the inside as brightly as possible, and keep the outside plain so that the contrast will be greater when they open the card up.

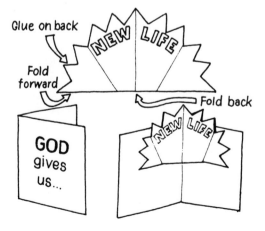

Children of God and Friends of Jesus

Things to Read

Deuteronomy 7:6-11
Galatians 3:23-4:7
John 15:12-17

Things to Do

Have on display a selection of things we are given by God which make life possible and enjoyable:

- a glass of water
- lump of coal
- salt
- pictures of a sunrise or sunset
- picture of rain
- plants and flowers

Talk about how much God must love us to give us all these, and many more they can add. Then sing a 'thank you' song.

Now present them with a problem. If they lent a friend one of their toys, and the friend did not use it properly, and broke it, how would they feel? Angry? Upset? What might they do? Take it back? Not lend them anything again? Hit them? (You could write the main points of this discussion up on a board or sheet.)

Then show them some pictures of people spoiling God's world and each other; children quarrelling, being unkind and destructive, people starving while others feast, the aftermath of a bomb explosion etc.

Explain that God sees us all spoiling what he has given us. He feels just as angry and upset, and he could, if he wanted, take the gifts away. As you say this, take away the water, sunlight etc, until the table is bleak and bare.

Why do you think he doesn't do that? Because he loves us so much, even when we are horrid. He hates what we do, sometimes, but he never hates us.

Let the children help put back all the lovely things. If God loves us that much, we must love each other that much.

Things to Sing

Think of a world without any flowers *(Come and Praise)*
God made the earth *(Wake up, World!)*
I'm black, I'm white, I'm short, I'm tall *(Wake up, World!)*
God is making a wonderful world *(Wake up, World!)*
Jesus had all kinds of friends *(Wake up, World!)*
Out to the great wide world we go *(Wake up, World!)*

Churches, Temples and People

Things to Read

1 Kings 8:22-30
1 Corinthians 3:10-17
John 2:13-22

Things to Do

Bring along a household repair manual which has clear diagrams in it, a piece of sandpaper for each child and an assortment of wood offcuts or driftwood, and plenty of varnish.

First show the children how important it is to prepare a wall before you paint it – otherwise the paint will not last. Show them how cracks need to be cleaned out before they can be filled and wood sanded down before it is varnished. Explain how repentance is the necessary cleaning out and preparation before any growing can start in our Christian lives. This is made clearer if you have a chart with diagrams similar to the repair manual like this:

Give the children a chart to use in prayer during the week, which helps them review areas in their lives which need to be sanded down or cleaned up for Christ to make beautiful and useful.

Now let the children select a piece of wood and sand it down smoothly before varnishing it. It may be used as an ornament, or a paper weight.

Things to Sing

God is making a wonderful world *(Wake up, World!)*
Jesus had all kinds of friends *(Wake up, World!)*
Out to the great wide world we go *(Wake up, World!)*

Jesus is Alive!

Things to Read

Isaiah 12
Isaiah 43:16-21
Matthew 28:1-10

Things to Do

Read the resurrection story to the children. You may prefer to read it from a children's version such as *Jesus is Risen* (*Palm Tree Bible* Series) or *Dead and Alive Again* which can be found both as a story and as a simple drama in *Wonderful World!* (Kevin Mayhew). As the story is told, it could be enacted using plasticine models on a tray with a stone 'cave' built on it in a garden.

Give each child a margarine tub with oasis in it, a selection of spring flowers and a tall white candle. Help them make an arrangement of joy at Jesus being alive forever. When they have finished, light all the candles and carry them in procession around the church, finally placing them either at the front or on the windowsills.

Things to Sing

You can't pin Jesus down *(Wake up, World!)*
Lord of the dance
Out to the great wide world we go *(Wake up, World!)*

FAITH, TRUST AND HOPE

Courage and Commitment

Things to Read

Daniel 3:13-26
Romans 8:18-25
Luke 9:51-end

Things to Do

Tell the children the story of Shadrach, Meshach and Abed-nego bringing out their determination to do what they know God wants them to do, even when it puts them in danger. Then help them to make this moving model of the three men in the fire out of card, a lolly stick, sticky tape and colouring pens.

Things to Sing

Lord of the dance
One more step along the world I go
Pick up your feet and go! *(Wake up, World!)*
He's got the whole world in his hand *(Come and Praise)*

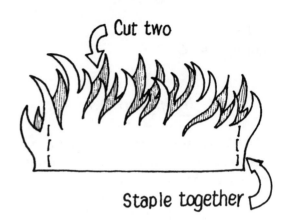

Cut two

Staple together

lolly stick

Faith and Works

Things to Read

Luke 20:9-17
James 2:14-26

Things to Do

First show some pictures of people in different uniforms (nurses, soldiers, brownies, astronauts, etc.) and ask the children what each person is.

Have the labels ready and stick them on to the pictures as each is named. Talk about what we know about each one because of the uniform worn. (We know, for instance, that the nurse probably works in a hospital, takes temperatures, gives out medicine and changes bandages etc.)

Then show an ordinary group of people. They are Christians (put on label) but their uniform is not their clothes – it is the way they behave. We can't see their faith, but we can see the effect of their faith, in their behaviour.

Discuss with the children what marks a person as being a Christian who has faith in God. (They worship God, pray, behave lovingly, forgive quickly, are happy even when they don't get everything their own way, they are helpful and kind etc.)

Point out that often we don't behave like this, and then we are letting God down, just as a nurse would let the hospital and the patients down if he or she didn't give out the right medicines. If we say we believe in God then we must show our faith in the way we act.

Now read them the first paragraph of the reading from James 2, first dressing one child up in rags with a begging bowl, so that you call across to this child, 'Good luck to you,' etc. at the appropriate time. Afterwards collect ideas for how a person with real faith in God would help, and act this out.

Organise an event during the week in which they can all help someone in a practical way.

Suggestions:
- clearing leaves from paths of elderly people
- a sponsored silence in aid of a charity
- a visit to an old people's home to sing to the residents and chat to them

Things to Sing

Keep on travelling on *(Wake up, World!)*
Out to the great wide world we go *(Wake up, World!)*
God is making a wonderful world *(Wake up, World!)*

Abraham's Faith

Things to Read

Genesis 12:1-9
John 8:51-end
Romans 4:13-end

Things to Do

First show the children a world map. Establish one or two countries they know of and then point out Haran and the route to Canaan. Also show pictures of the landscape there (the local library should have some books with photographs of the Bible lands). It is important that the children realise these places really exist!

Now tell the children about a man who lived there, called Abraham. Read them just the first paragraph of the Genesis reading. Talk together about how it feels to be starting out somewhere new for the first time, such as a new school, a new class or moving house. Abraham, too, may well have been a bit scared. He may not have particularly wanted to go. But he trusted God and obeyed him. God promised that he would be with Abraham and he kept his word.

Using an old baking tray, sand and stones, make a model of Abraham setting off for the promised land. Abraham and his family are made of pipecleaners and pieces of material, and sheep and goats are made from black and white pipe-cleaners. Write a title for the model:

ABRAHAM TRUSTED GOD

Things to Sing

One more step along the world I go
  (Come and Praise)
Abraham! *(Wake up, World!)*
Keep on travelling on *(Wake up, World!)*
Pick up your feet and go *(Wake up, World!)*

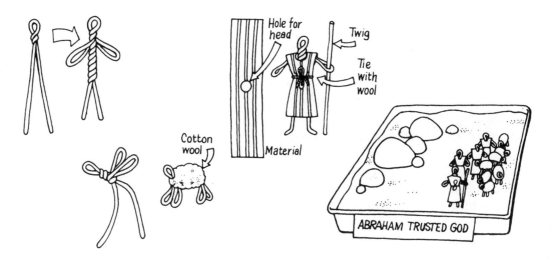

Faith and Prayer

Things to Read

Luke 11:1-13
Ephesians 3:14-end

Things to Do

Talk with the children about asking. Suppose they would like a friend round to play or some help with a tricky model they are building, what would they do? Ask Mummy and Daddy, and if they can help, they will. It's no good just thinking to ourselves, 'If only I could have my friend to play.' We have to ask, and then we've got a good chance of our hopes coming true. (At this stage show the first sign: 'Ask and you will receive.') Point out that it's the same with our heavenly Father; it's no good just thinking to ourselves, 'If only I didn't get bad-tempered so often!' or 'If only I wasn't so scared of owning up!' But if we ASK our heavenly Father, he will help us to change!

Have ready hidden an object in the room. Tell the children something is hidden. How can they find it? By looking! (Let them hunt till they find it. Then show the second sign: 'Seek and you will find.') Point out that in the same way we will never find out about Jesus, or ourselves or other people unless we get up and make an effort to find out, by reading the Bible, asking people, thinking and being aware.

Show a picture of a front door. How can you get someone to open it? By knocking or ringing the bell – no one will answer unless you do! (Show third sign: ' Knock and the door will be opened to you.') It is the same with God, our Father. He is there, alive, strong and he likes us – in fact, he loves us! But he will never push into our lives; if we want his help, or if we want to know about his way of living, we must ASK, SEEK and KNOCK at the door.

Let three groups colour and decorate the three signs, to be put in church where everyone can see them. Then join in prayer together, encouraging the children to add their prayers too.

Things to Sing

I'm black, I'm white, I'm short, I'm tall *(Wake up, World!)*
Keep on travelling on *(Wake up, World!)*
Break the bread and pour the wine *(Wake up, World!)*

God's Mysterious Spirit

Things to Read

Exodus 19:16-25
John 14:15-26
Acts 2:1-21

A children's version of this story, entitled *Wind and Fire*, is published by Kevin Mayhew.

Things to Do

Tell the children what happened at Pentecost, emphasising that Jesus' friends were keeping in touch with him through prayer, so they were prepared when his life, or Spirit, came to them so powerfully. Explain that we need to keep in touch with him, too, if we want him to live in us.

Talk about qualities the Holy Spirit gives us – love, joy, peace etc. Then help the children to make long streamers out of orange, red and yellow, with these qualities drawn or printed on them. As the children come into church they dance round the aisles waving the streamers and twirling them so they look like fire.

Things to Sing

Kum ba yah
Pick up your feet and go *(Wake up, World!)*
Out to the great wide world we go *(Wake up, World!)*

Faith Without Seeing

Things to Read

John 20:19-29
1 Peter 1:3-9

A children's version of the gospel story, as both narrative and drama, entitled *I'll Believe It When I See It*, can be found in *Wonderful World!* (Kevin Mayhew).

Things to Do

Begin by passing round a 'feeling' bag with a couple of objects inside it, such as a sieve and a marble, for instance. Each child has a turn to feel the bag and guess what the objects are, but the guesses aren't shared until everyone has had a go.

Then each one says: 'I believe there's a . . . in the bag'. Take the objects out to see who's right, and talk about how they didn't know for sure what was there until they saw it, but they could believe it by using clues, such as what it felt like.

Display a large sign: 'I believe Jesus is God's Son.'

How do we know?

Have we actually seen him?

What clues do we use, then?

Talk about the record of his friends in the Bible; the way Jesus helps us to be kind when we feel like being nasty, (so long as we ask him); the way he helps us through sad or painful times; and the happy feeling we have when we enjoy the lovely world with him.

Then read the gospel story and give the children a picture to colour.

Things to Sing

You can't pin Jesus down *(Wake up, World!)*
One more step along the world I go *(Come and Praise)*
Keep on travelling on *(Wake up, World!)*

God Turns Sorrow into Joy

Things to Read

Isaiah 25:6-9
Luke 24:13-35
Revelation 19:6-9

A children's version of the gospel story, as both narrative and drama, entitled *A Stranger on the Road*, can be found in *Wonderful World!* (Kevin Mayhew).

Things to Do

Read the story, and talk about it with the children:

- why do they think the disciples couldn't believe Jesus had risen?
- do they sometimes wonder if it is all true, and then later feel certain of Jesus being with them?
- talk about having expectations (for Christmas presents, for instance) which make us feel let down when they are not what we had in mind.
- when have they been surprised by God acting in their lives?

Teachers can give great encouragement in faith by being prepared to talk about some of their own surprises and disappointments; the children are then brought into contact with the real, living faith, rather than history. Help the children make this pop-up scene of Jesus breaking bread.

Things to Sing

You shall go out with joy *(Songs and Hymns of Fellowship)*
Out to the great wide world we go *(Wake up, World!)*
Break the bread and pour the wine *(Wake up, World!)*
Jesus turned the water into wine *(Wake up, World!)*

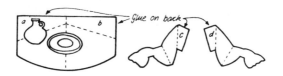

God's Way is Different – and Better!

Things to Read

Matthew 5:1-12
1 Corinthians 4:8-13

Things to Do

Bring along an assortment of advertisements mounted on a board so the children can see them as they come in. You could have some on tape as well from television and radio.

Why do firms advertise? So as to get us to buy their product. Every day we are encouraged to WANT and to GET. The more we GET, the more we WANT. Stick a thin strip of paper over the advertisements which says: GET, GET, GET. WANT, WANT, WANT. GET, GET, GET all across it.

But if *things* are most important in our life, they make life harder, not happier. Have some heavy chains, stonefilled bags with straps etc. with labels on such as:

– I wish I could have . . .
– If only I could . . .
– I want . . .
– Leave that alone – it's MINE.

One by one, hang them around yourself or a child who volunteers, until he is really loaded down. Jesus says to us: 'Trust in me, instead of in THINGS. You'll find you're much happier.'

Then remove the chains and burdens and replace them with an 'I'm for Jesus' badge. Let the volunteer demonstrate how much easier it now is to move and run about without all that cumbersome clutter.

When we trust in Jesus we can enjoy what we are given, but also enjoy giving away. We can enjoy owning, but also enjoy sharing. We can be happy when we have lots of toys, but also be happy when we haven't got many.

Let the children make an 'I'm for Jesus' badge to wear, and ask them to try giving instead of getting at least once each day this week.

Things to Sing

Out to the great wide world we go *(Wake up, World!)*
He was born in the winter *(Wake up, World!)*
God made the earth *(Wake up, World!)*

Healing and Wholeness

Things to Read

2 Kings 5:1-14
Mark 7:24-end
2 Corinthians 12:1-10

A children's version of the Old Testament story, entitled *Naaman's Spots*, is available in the *Palm Tree Bible* series (Kevin Mayhew).

Things to Sing

He's got the whole world in his hand
  (Come and Praise)
Lord of the dance
God is making a wonderful world *(Wake up, World!)*

Things to Do

Read *Naamam's Spots*, or another version of the story with pictures, and then go through the story again with the children acting it out. A narrator holds everything together, and children not involved as main characters are servants and interested onlookers.

Children are often very good at praying for others, and are helped by pictures. Explain to them how important their prayers are in making people better, and help them make a praying scrap book. On the first page they stick a picture of Jesus healing someone, and on the others they will be drawing, or sticking in pictures and photographs of any prayer needs for healing. These may be from newspapers and magazines, snapshots etc. Encourage the children to use their books regularly, and from time to time give them the name or picture of others who need their prayers. This becomes beneficial in both directions – the elderly, sick or lonely in the parish gain great support from knowing the child is praying for them, and the child is learning unselfish prayer and a deeper friendship with Jesus.

Hope and Pray

Things to Read

Habakkuk 2:1-4
Acts 26:1-8
Luke 18:1-8

Things to Do

Talk with the children about working hard at something until at last it is finished. They may have found it difficult making a model, mixing a cake, tidying their bedroom or learning to swim or skip, for instance.

You could bring to show them something you had to persevere with, such as a knitted jumper, loaf of bread, or piece of music, and tell them you sometimes wanted to stop and give up, but decided not to.

Help them to see that perseverance is not always easy, but it is always worthwhile.

Now tell the story of Moses, using plasticine models or pictures to illustrate it.

Give each child a card to split into days and with a prayer they have made up to say every day. Perhaps their parents might like to say it with them.

Ask them to bring their cards back next week with a tick drawn each day they remembered to do it.

Things to Sing

Keep on travelling on *(Wake up, World!)*
In the winter nights are dark *(Wake up, World!)*
Out to the great wide world we go *(Wake up, World!)*
Pick up your feet and go *(Wake up, World!)*

Our God reigns

Things to Read

Daniel 7:9-14
Acts 1:3-11
Ephesians 1:15-end

Things to Do

It is not widely known that children are still entitled to take time off from school on Ascension Day in order to go to church. If you decide to have a special children's service, make out a form for the children to take into school and use the occasion to witness through courtesy and goodwill.

Keep the service simple and involve the children in the planning, reading, singing and decorating.

Start by showing the children a bright cut-out sun, then cover it from sight with a cut-out cloud. Is the sun still there? Show that it is. We do not always see it because it is sometimes hidden from view, but we know it is always there. How?

Talk about life and growth and light and warmth. If we shut ourselves in where the sun couldn't reach us we wouldn't survive. Can we see Jesus? No. Then what do we mean when we say he is alive? Where is he?

Read them the account of the Ascension as told in Acts. His friends had seen him a lot after he had come back to life on the first Easter Day, and now, like the sun behind a cloud, he is hidden from sight for a time. (Show a bright card with JESUS written on it, and put the cloud in front.) But he is just as much alive as before. As our King he reigns over everything – people, animals, the sun, the stars, the universe!

Ask some children to draw and colour flowers and trees, some animals and people, some stars and planets, mountains, seas and weather. Then mount all their work on a big collage banner, with OUR GOD REIGNS written over the top. This can be carried into the church in procession.

Things to Sing

He's got the whole world in his hand *(Come and Praise)*
Out to the great wide world we go *(Wake up, World!)*
You can't pin Jesus down *(Wake up, World!)*

The Hope of Heaven

Things to Read

2 Kings 2:1-15
Luke 24:45-end
Ephesians 4:1-13

Things to Do

In an effort to steer clear of false impressions, we sometimes avoid teaching children about heaven. Here is a good opportunity to put that right. Start with a game. In a box have slips of paper which describe things in terms of other things:

- a bit like an orange but not so sweet, and coloured yellow;
- a kind of chair which has no back;
- a tall sort of cup;
- a wax stick that you can burn slowly; etc.

Point out that if you had not known before what a lemon was, you would have a better idea now, but not an exact idea until you actually saw a lemon yourself. Show them one. And similarly with the other items described.

It is the same with heaven. Pictures and words in the Bible give us clues but no more.

Show a large round poster with these words written all round the edge:

Heaven is where Jesus is.

Then make a collection of words inside the circle which give us an idea of what heaven is like:

- happy
- beauty
- peace
- joy
- no worry

- Daddy finds you when you were lost
- like when you give Nana your best drawing and she's very pleased
- like when your friends ask you to join in their game, etc.

Stress that these are only clues, but try to show them some idea of what being with Jesus means in feelings they can understand, rather than looking at the idea of 'place'.

Let the children decorate the words with lovely bright colours and patterns and if possible display the poster in church.

Things to Sing

Give me oil in my lamp
You shall go out with joy *(Songs and Hymns of Fellowship)*
One more step along the world I go *(Come and Praise)*

52

Stand Firm

Things to Read

Matthew 7:13-27
1 Peter 2:4-7

Things to Do

Bring along two sets of building bricks (not interlocking ones). Divide the children into two groups and let each build a house. One is based on a firm block of wood, the other on a thick layer of sand in a tray.

When both are finished, tell the children Jesus' story of the two houses. At the point of the stormy rain, pour water round the bases of each in turn. The sand will cave in and the 'rock' will not.

Make sure you explain what Jesus told the story for, or they will not understand. Point out how silly it was not to have a good strong foundation, (they may have seen houses being built with foundations deep in the ground) and that we can choose to build our lives on strong rock or slipping sand.

Things to Sing

I'm gonna build my life
He's got the whole world in his hand
(Come and Praise)
I'm black, I'm white, I'm short, I'm tall
(Wake up, World!)
Out to the great wide world we go *(Wake up, World!)*

Build on God – put him first

Living by Faith

Things to Read

Genesis 28:10-end
Matthew 6:24-end
Hebrews 11:1-2, 8-16

Things to Do

Make up a story about Mr Worry-a-lot, illustrating it with flannelgraph pictures. He might worry about what he's going to wear, what he's going to eat, who he's going to invite, where he should go on holiday etc.

Then he meets Mr Trust, who finds him in a bad state of nerves. One by one he sorts out Mr Worry-a-lot's problems with him, showing him that he is worrying unnecessarily because God is sure to look after him. When the next worry arises, they remember to stop and ask God to help them and are then much happier, knowing that God will not let them down. You could make the characters look something like this:

Mr Worry-a-lot   Mr Trust

and give the children cut-outs of each character to colour in and take home.

Things to Sing

God knows me *(Come and Praise)*
He's got the whole world in his hand *(Come and Praise)*
Abraham! *(Wake up, World!)*
Keep on travelling on *(Wake up, World!)*
We can plough and dig the land *(Wake up, World!)*

God Changes Lives

Things to Read

Daniel 6:10-22
Luke 19:1-10

Both these stories are available, both as stories and as dramas, in *Wonderful World!* (Kevin Mayhew). where they are called the *First Lion Tamer* and *Jesus and the Tax Man.*

Things to Do

Both the Daniel and the Zacchaeus stories provide excellent teaching material.

After the reading make a model of the story on a base, such as an old tray. Use modelling clay for the figures (and the lions), twigs stuck in cotton reels with tissue paper leaves for trees, painted boxes for houses, sandpaper and stones for the terrain. Bring the finished models in to display in the church with the heading:

Trust in God can change your life!

Things to Sing

God knows me *(Come and Praise)*
He's got the whole world in his hand *(Come and Praise)*
Jesus had all kinds of friends *(Wake up, World!)*
Out to the great wide world we go *(Wake up, World!)*

Keeping Hope Alive

Things to Read

Deuteronomy 34
John 16:12-24
Romans 8:35-end

Things to Do

Talk with the children about how we can keep in touch with people when they are in different places; for example: radio, telephone, fax, letters. Talk about when these aids are used for space travel, docking a ship, in aeroplanes, or at other times when it would be dangerous to act without the guidance of someone who can see better than we can, and who knows all the relevant information.

In life, God is at the base control, and can see the whole picture of what is happening – not just our little bit of it. He is able and willing to guide us through and stay in close contact all the time. Now show them a telephone. What do we have to do to get in touch with someone at the other end of the line? Explain that although God is always in touch with us, we won't be able to talk to him and listen to him unless we keep in touch from our end, too. And that's what praying is.

Help the children make yoghurt pot telephones. Write on them at one end: 'Don't forget to keep in touch with God' and at the other end: 'God always listens'.

Things to Sing

One more step along the world I go
(Come and Praise)
Give me oil in my lamp
He's got the whole world in his hand
(Come and Praise)

TEMPTATION, SIN, FORGIVENESS

Loving and Forgiving

Things to Read

Colossians 3:12-17
Luke 15:11-end

A children's version of this story is available, as both narrative and drama, entitled *Whatever You've Done, I Love You*, in *Wonderful World!* (Kevin Mayhew).

Things to Sing

Whatever you've done, I love you *(Wonderful World!)*
Jesus had all kinds of friends *(Wake up, World!)*
Out to the great wide world we go *(Wake up, World!)*

Things to Do

The prodigal son is a lovely story to act out. Have a large assortment of dressing up clothes available (curtains, net, lengths of material, old ties and towels etc.)
Tell the children the story, showing pictures of the son:
   (a)   asking for money;
   (b)   waving goodbye;
   (c)   spending it all;
   (d)   as a pig keeper;
   (e)   returning to his father's welcome.
The elder brother can be omitted with young children as there is plenty for them to grasp without it, and it may make the lesson too complicated.
   (f)   Angry   brother   with   father explaining.
Having given parts (plenty can be servants, girl friends and pigs) read out the story bit by bit while the children act it out.
   The value of this type of drama is in the involvement, rather than the standard of performance, so suggest what the characters might say as you go along.

Ready and Waiting

Things to Read

Luke 12:35-40
Ephesians 6:10-18

Things to Do

Bring in a box of pencils or crayons, most of which are blunt or broken. (In my experience such collections are easy to find!) Ask two or three children to pick out of the box the pencils and crayons which are sharp and unbroken. Out of all that box only a very few were still in a good state. Explain today's readings by referring to the pencils. In a way we are like the pencils, except that we are able to go and get ourselves sharpened and cleaned up when we need to. (Saying sorry to God when we have been selfish or unkind, and making an effort to put things right again.) We can also choose not to bother. But we never know when God is wanting to use us, and if we have let ourselves get into a bad state, he won't be able to use us very easily. It's not enough to be a pencil – we need to be SHARPENED pencils.

On a chart or blackboard write down some ways we can make sure we are keeping ourselves ready. Here are some suggestions, but the children will have ideas as well:

Talking to Jesus and listening to him

Reading the Bible and learning from it

Putting things right quickly when we do wrong

Forgiving people when they hurt us or spoil our toys.

Give the children a new pencil each and help them make this pencil-end for it.

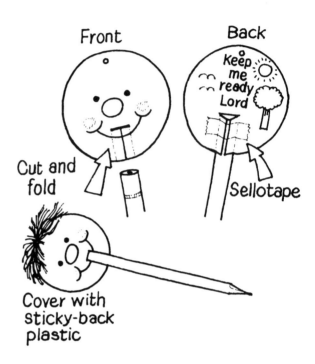

While they work, pass round some pencil sharpeners and let each child sharpen one of the blunt pencils.

Things to Sing

Give me oil in my lamp
God is making a wonderful world *(Wake up, world!)*
Kum ba yah

Forgiveness

Things to Read

1 Samuel 24:1-17
Luke 7:36-end
Galatians 6:1-10

Things to Do

Tell this story, like the one Jesus told Simon, using the children to help you. First choose a postman, and give him a bag and badge (or hat) with two bills to deliver.

'One morning the postman delivered a letter to Sam Butcher. (Postman gives one bill to him.) Sam opened it (let him open it and show everyone) and inside was a bill for £5.

How do you think Sam felt? A bit fed up/miserable? "At least it's not too big a bill," he thought. "I'll have to go without all my sweets this week."

Then the postman delivered a letter to Robert South. (He delivers it.) Robert opened it and looked inside. It was a bill for £5000!

How do you think Robert felt? He was very worried and sad, because he didn't have much money at all. "Oh dear," he thought, "I'll never manage to pay this. Not unless I sell my house – and then where could I live?"

He felt worried and sad all day. He hardly slept that night, for thinking about the way he couldn't pay that huge bill. Perhaps he would be sent to prison, even.

Next morning the postman delivered another letter to Sam and another to Robert. They opened them, rather nervously. Inside was an important looking letter. It said (let the children read it our together)

Dear Sir,
I am going to let you off.
You need not pay me
the money after all.
Best wishes,
Tom Smith (Manager).

Well, how do you think they felt? Happy/delighted/relieved? They felt very relieved and happy. Sam was glad he could buy some sweets as usual.

But who do you think felt most thankful? It was Robert! He had been so worried and sad, and it was as if a great heavy weight was lifted off him. He ran out to Tom Smith's office to thank him straight away. He would never forget Tom's kindness.'

Explain that Jesus is rather like Tom Smith, and we are like Sam and Robert. When we do something wrong or unkind it is like being in debt. When we are forgiven, our debt is paid, and we feel happy and relieved again. Let the children make these cards to remind them.

Things to Sing

God is making a wonderful world (*Wake up, World!*)
Out to the great wide world we go (*Wake up, World!*)

Seventy Times Seven

Things to Read

Hosea 11:1-9
Matthew 18:21-end
1 Corinthians 13

A children's version of the parable of the unforgiving servant, in both narrative and dramatic form and entitled *(Come On, Cough Up!* can be found in *Wonderful World!* (Kevin Mayhew).

Things to Sing

Jesus had all kinds of friends *(Wake up, World!)*
Out to the great wide world we go *(Wake up, World!)*

Things to Do

Begin by asking them the question Peter asked Jesus – how often do they think they should forgive their brothers and sisters if they keep irritating breaking toys/teasing etc. It will probably become clear that there is quite a gap between ideals and reality, so help them to be honest!

Then tell them how Peter asked Jesus the same question and how he explained his answer with a story. Tell the story, using different headgear for the various characters, some bills and play money and a pair of handcuffs, or something similar. You can grab hold of a volunteer when the second servant is nearly throttled. If the children have enjoyed an entertaining telling of the story, and been involved in it, they will remember it more.

So having told it and talked about what it says about the way we should behave, let all the children join in an acted version.

The Cost of Love and Forgiveness

Things to Read

Isaiah 52:13-53:12
John 18:1-19:37

Things to Do

It is important that children are able to walk their own 'Way of the Cross' today. One way of making this possible is to organise a one or two hour session of teaching, singing and craft activities, with a break for hot cross buns and a drink. A possible programme might be:

10.00 a.m. Introduction with brief talk (*What happened on Good Friday*), prayer and a song.

10.25 a.m. Begin activities

10.45 a.m. Break: drink and hot cross bun

11.00 a.m. Resume and complete activities

11.20 a.m. Gather for short litany, and a song and blessing

11.30 a.m. End

Possible activities:

a. Make a Holy Week frieze with the crowd, the crosses and the tomb;

b. Make a smaller banner for taking home. Have background material already stitched and figure shapes out of felt. The children assemble it with glue, and thread two sticks through top and bottom, with a piece of wool to hang it up. These could perhaps be blessed at the end.

c. A standing cross could be made from wood. Have ready the base blocks and cross pieces. The children sand the wood down, glue and nail together and varnish. N.B. Very careful supervision necessary!

d. Blow eggs (pierce both ends with a needle, and blow contents into a bowl). Then decorate on them a cross made of flowers, coloured with felt tip pens. Use this as a symbol of Christ's death bringing new life. Make a holder for the egg from a small box covered and stuck with coloured paper, and filled with cotton wool.

The atmosphere should be calm and quiet, with the activities being looked on as part of their worship.

Things to Sing

Lord of the Dance
Kum ba yah
When I needed a neighbour (*Come and Praise*)

Jesus Wipes Away Sins

Things to Read

John 8:2-11
Colossians 1:18-23

A children's version of the gospel story, both as narrative and drama, entitled *Living in Glass Houses* can be found in *Wonderful World!* (Kevin Mayhew).

Things to Do

Read or act out the gospel story.

Have a blackboard, coloured chalk, and an effective board rubber. Have an old dirty sack or bag labelled SINS in nasty looking letters. Inside have separate cards – jagged and irregular, on which are written:
- telling lies;
- stealing;
- pushing someone over;
- spoiling someone's toys; etc.

Ask one child to scatter them all around, and each picks one up. Each is written on the blackboard.

Explain how Jesus can wipe them right out, if we are really sorry. (Now rub them out.) How do we show we are sorry?

Let the children draw a beautiful picture on the blackboard for Jesus, and bring it into church.

Things to Sing

God forgave my sins in Jesus' name
  (Songs and Hymns of Fellowship)
Out to the great wide world we go *(Wake up, World!)*
You shall go out with joy *(Songs and Hymns of Fellowship)*

Honest Worship

Things to Read

Jeremiah 7:1-11
John 4:19-26
Hebrews 12:18-end

Things to Do

Talk about being honest with God: saying our prayers and then being unkind, lazy or boastful, for instance. Explain that this is really lying, and we need to make it up with Jesus by saying we are sorry and having him forgive us – which he ALWAYS will. Have a short prayer time to do this.

Tell the children how God makes our lives beautiful and then builds us into his living church. Give each child an ordinary-looking muddy stone. Have ready several bowls of soapy water and kitchen roll, with protective aprons and scrubbing brushes. The children clean and decorate their stones and then arrange them on an outline of a cross. Nightlights can be placed among the stones. Gather round this cross to sing to Jesus some praise songs.

Things to Sing

Break the bread and pour the wine *(Wake up, World!)*
God is making a wonderful world *(Wake up, World!)*
Out to the great wide world we go *(Wake up, World!)*

Listen to God!

Things to Read

Genesis 6:11-end

A children's version of this story, both as a narrative and as a drama, entitled *A Boatful of Trouble* is available in *Wonderful World!* (Kevin Mayhew). The *Palm Tree Bible* version of the story is called *Noah's Big Boat.*

Help the children make this ark to remind them.

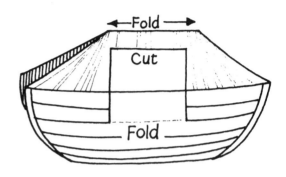

Things to Do

Show the children some pictures from traditional stories where it is very obvious who is the good character and who is the bad one. You could have a thumbs up sign whenever you point to a 'goodie' and a hiss whenever the 'baddie' appears. Then talk with them about how much harder it often is in real life to decide what is good and what is evil. Think, for instance, of when you make yourself late for school (hiss for bad) because you stopped to help at a bicycle accident (thumbs up for good), or when you offer to carry the shopping (thumbs up) so Dad won't notice a bar of chocolate you have stolen (hiss).

So how can we know for certain what is right and wrong? If you have the recording of Pinnochio, play and sing along with Jimminy Cricket, the voice of conscience. Through our conscience, God shows us which way is right, but we have to listen hard, or we may not hear. When we pray about a problem, Jesus will guide us through it safely. That's what Noah did, and he and his family were brought safely through the flood.

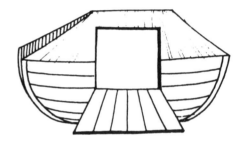

Things to Sing

All of the creatures God had made (*Wake up, World!*)
Keep on travelling on (*Wake up, World!*)

Taking Responsibility

Things to Read

Genesis 2:7-9; 3:1-7
Matthew 4:1-11
Hebrews 2:14-end

Things to Do

Tell the children the story of Adam and Eve explaining that it was their disobedience which cut them off from the happy life they had before with God. Then help them make a large collage picture of the garden with the tree of knowledge in the middle. Make sure all the other trees have lovely fruit as well as this one; there was, after all, no actual need for them to eat its fruit. Use lots of bright materials, or colours cut from magazine pages, and write on the picture 'Adam and Eve did not do as God told them. That spoilt things.' Then give them two large twigs each and make them into a simple cross. This is another tree of life. Help them to see how Jesus did obey, even though it meant he was killed. Because he obeyed, he put everything right again. So now, if we do wrong, we can be completely forgiven, all because of Jesus.

Use a prayer of penitence and thanks for forgiveness.

> Heavenly Father,
> we are very sorry
> that we have hurt you
> and each other
> and spoilt your world.
> Thank you for sending Jesus
> to put things right.
> Please forgive us
> because of his goodness.   Amen

Things to Sing

Think of a world without any flowers *(Come and Praise)*
Blame somebody else *(Wake up, World!)*
God is making a wonderful world *(Wake up, World!)*
Out to the great wide world we go *(Wake up, World!)*

Falling Away from Goodness

Things to Read

Genesis 4:1-16
Mark 7:14-23
1 John 3:9-18

Things to Do

Remind the children of the beautiful world God has made and then talk with them about the way we all sometimes spoil it. Have ready a display of pictures to help the thinking. Cut some from newspapers, or use these drawings:

Tell the children the story of how Cain started off being mean and ungrateful to God, became jealous of his brother, began to hate his brother and eventually killed him. Slide a stone down a tilted tray to show how easy it is to slide down once you've got started. Perhaps they have tried stopping halfway down a slide – it takes a lot of strength.

What can we do to stop ourselves slipping down into sin? Show them a large rolled strip of paper and ask one child to hold an end while another child unrolls it. The others read out what it says:

HOLD ON TIGHT TO JESUS!

We can talk to Jesus about our bad habits and ask him to help us change them.

We can call to him for strength when we feel tempted to be greedy, unkind or bad-tempered.

We can try to form new habits, such as being helpful, friendly or generous.

Pray together, thanking God for his gifts to us through the last week, asking his forgiveness for times we have spoilt his world, and offering him the coming week for God to use us to spread his love around.

Colour in the letters on the strip of paper and display it in church.

Things to Sing

Love is something if you give it away
When I needed a neighbour (Hymns Old and New)
God said, 'Cain, where is your brother?' (Wake up, World!)

WORSHIP, DISCIPLESHIP, MISSION

Good Neighbours

Things to Read

Leviticus 19:9-end
Luke 10:25-37
Romans 12:9-end

A children's version of the gospel story, both as narrative and as drama, entitled *Neighbours*, can be found in *Wonderful World!* (Kevin Mayhew).

Things to Sing

Love is something if you give it away
I'm black, I'm white, I'm short, I'm tall *(Wake up, World!)*
God is making a wonderful world *(Wake up, World!)*
When I needed a neighbour *(Come and Praise)*

Things to Do

The Good Samaritan is an excellent story for the children to act out, but it needs to be clearly explained first.

If the priest and the Levite touched a dead man they would be considered 'unclean' by the Law. The man looked dead, so they passed by, pretending they hadn't noticed.

The Samaritan came from another country so it was extra strange for him to bother with the man. But because he saw the man needed help he felt sorry for him, and helped him as best he could.

There are several book versions of the story which can be used. Give the children lots of help with what to do and say, setting out the room first with a road, an inn, Jerusalem and Jericho. Have strips of material for bandages and some pretend ointment in a small pot, some play money in a bag and some plastic cups for the people at the inn.

Love in Action

Things to Read

Deuteronomy 15:7-11
Luke 16:19-end
1 John 4:15-end

Things to Do

Make a display board of something like the Clean Water project, or Famine relief, tree planting and mud stoves or a sponsored village.

Supply bright background paper and pictures from newspapers and magazines. Many of the relief organisations are happy to supply excellent material: a selection of addresses is below.

Begin the session with a song of thanks.

Then tell the story that Jesus told about the rich man and Lazarus, and follow up last week's activities for helping before arranging this week's display.

Make it as clear as possible by headings, questions and maps. Coloured wool pinned between areas of the map and relevant information may be helpful.

Display the board where the rest of the congregation can see it, possibly bringing it in at the offertory.

Useful Addresses

Action Aid, 208 Upper Street, London N1 1RZ

Christian Aid, P.O. Box 1, London SW9 8BH

Oxfam, 274 Banbury Road, Oxford OX2 7DZ

Traidcraft, Kingsway, Gateshead NE11 0NE

U.S.P.G., Partnership House, 157 Waterloo Road, London SE1 8XA

V.S.O., 9 Belgrave Square, London SW1X 8PW

Things to Sing

Love is something if you give it away
I'm black, I'm white, I'm short, I'm tall *(Wake up, World!)*
God is making a wonderful world *(Wake up, World!)*
When I needed a neighbour *(Come and Praise)*

Choosing God's Way

Things to Read

Deuteronomy 11:18-28
Luke 16:1-9

Things to Do

First give the children a maze to do, individually with a pencil. Here is one you could use:

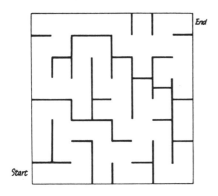

Talk about what happens when they go down a dead end:
– they are out of the main route
– they can't make any progress
– the only way out is to retrace their steps
– if they just stay there they may be imprisoned with no freedom.

Now show them a large picture of the maze either on a blackboard or sheet of card. The beginning of our maze, as Christians, is when we are baptised. (Stick a picture of baptism, or a font at the start of the maze.)

All the time we go on the right route we are putting Jesus first. In his love we can enjoy loving Mum and Dad, playing with brothers and sisters, enjoy football, painting, going on holiday, helping Nana, having friends to tea etc. (Write these, and their ideas, in coloured pencil along the route, with a cross, as Jesus' sign, in between each one.) Because Jesus is Love, he helps us love and appreciate other people.

But suppose one thing starts to be more important than our love for Jesus? (Write one item, such as 'football' or 'having friends to tea' at a dead end.) It will cut us off from the supply of Love, and our lives will be stuck at a dead end. So what can we do if that happens? We have to go back the way we came, meet up with Jesus, and then we can live in his love again.

Things to Sing

One more step along the world I go
Keep on travelling on *(Wake up, World!)*
Pick up your feet and go *(Wake up, World!)*

God of Surprises

Things to Read

1 Kings 19:9-18
Matthew 24:37-44

Things to Do

Have ready three parcels, wrapped up in Christmas paper. They should all be the same size and shape – ask a shoe shop to let you have some shoe boxes. Inside one box place a lot of wadding, tissue or scrunched-up newspaper. In another box place a tiny jewellery box containing something precious, such as a gold ring, or a diamond. In the third, place a pair of shoes.

Talk with the children about preparing our parcels for Christmas, and the fun of surprises. It is exciting to see a parcel with our name on it and not know what is inside. Often it turns out to be different from what we expect. Now show them the three parcels. Do they think that because they look the same they will have the same things inside? Ask one child to undo the first parcel. At the shoe box stage, guess the contents. When they see all the paper they will still expect something to be tucked inside. It's a surprise to find nothing there. Ask another child to open the second parcel. At the shoe box stage this time some may still expect shoes. Others will expect nothing. This time the contents are much more precious than we expected. A third child opens the last parcel. Stop again at the shoe box stage. Very few will now expect shoes, so it comes as a surprise to find what would normally be expected in a shoe box.

God is full of surprises, too. Sometimes, sadly, we must expect to find him in the lives of people who claim to follow him, but their behaviour shows that he isn't there. (Perhaps others may not find him in OUR behaviour, sometimes.) At other times he surprises us by blessing us richly when we are not expecting it. (On a bad day, when everyone seems cross with you, your pet gives you a special welcome, perhaps.)

We need to keep looking out for God, not lust tucking him away into Sunday mornings. Otherwise, when he comes again we won't be ready for him. Read the last paragraph of today's gospel passage and pray together that God will help us all stay faithful in our lives.

Help the children make these traffic lights to remind them.

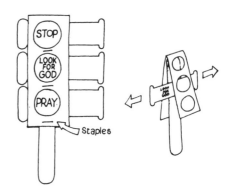

Things to Sing

Out to the great wide world we go (*Wake up, World!*)
God is making a wonderful world (*Wake up, World!*)

Hear God Calling

Things to Read

1 Samuel 3:1-10
John 1:35-end
Galatians 1:11-end

Things to Do

Tell the children the story of God calling to Samuel, involving two of them in the story to mime the events.

Now divide them into two groups to play a game. The children in one line are given a different short message which they have to shout across to their partner on the far side of the room. The trouble is that everyone will shout their message at the same time! See how long it takes before everyone has received the right message. Then gather everyone round in a circle and hold up a pin. Try to hear the pin drop. Once this stillness has been achieved, talk quietly with them about the need to be quiet and still in our prayer if we are to know what God wants us to do.

Finish with a time of prayer based on the sounds we can hear when we close our eyes and really listen. Pray for travellers and drivers when you hear traffic; for those with colds and others who are ill; for babies and those being born; thank God for the wind or the rain, and so on. Encourage the children to add their prayers; there is no better way to learn to pray than by praying.

Things to Sing

Kum ba yah
Out to the great wide world we go *(Wake up, World!)*
God is making a wonderful world *(Wake up, World!)*

God is Shown to the World

Things to Read

Isaiah 49:1-6
Matthew 2:1-12
Ephesians 3:1-12

A children's version of the gospel story, as both narrative and drama, entitled *Ride That Camel! Chase That Star!* can be found in *Wonderful World!* (Kevin Mayhew).

Things to Do

Tell or read the story of the wise men, with their gifts displayed on the table. If possible, have something of real gold, a thurible with incense burning, and some anointing oil. Talk about these things, and how we use them in our worship (or way of showing the "worth") of our God. How can we give God a present?

Wrap each child in Christmas wrapping paper and give each a label to write and decorate, thread on wool and hang round their neck. At the offering of gifts, let the 'presents' walk up to give themselves. The labels can be collected and blessed before they are returned to the children.

Things to Sing

Ride that camel! Chase that star! *(Wonderful World!)*
We three kings of orient are
Pick up your feet and go *(Wake up, World!)*
Out to the great wide world we go *(Wake up, World!)*
I'm black, I'm white, I'm short, I'm tall *(Wonderful World!)*

Offering and Sharing

Things to Read

Deuteronomy 8:1-6
John 6:1-14
Philippians 4:10-20

A children's version of the gospel story, as both narrative and drama, entitled *The Biggest Picnic in History*, can be found in *Wonderful World!* (Kevin Mayhew).

Things to Sing

Feed the hungry people *(Wake up, World!)*
When I needed a neighbour
Break the bread and pour the wine *(Wake up, World!)*
God is making a wonderful world *(Wake up, World!)*

Things to Do

Cut out from card five small rolls and two fish, colour them and put them in a lunch box, and use this as you tell the children today's gospel story. It will help them imagine it all better if you enlist their help in being the crowd walking round the lake, listening to Jesus' words, one boy being Philip and another the one who had a lunch box which he offered and so on.

Then help them make five barley loaves and two fish each, using the card ones as templates. On the back of each item write a word which can be shuffled into a prayer, like this:

Good will Overcome Evil

Things to Read

Hosea 6:1-6
John 16:25-end
1 Corinthians 15:21-28

Things to Do

Have ready an assortment of pictures and newspaper cuttings about good and bad things in our world. Talk with the children about some of the very good things in the world. Is it all good? What sort of bad things happen? (Wars, not enough food for some, quarrels, selfishness, crimes etc.) Read them the words of Jesus: 'In the world you will have trouble. But courage! The victory is mine; I have conquered the world.' So although there are bad things, and some of them will happen to us during life, God's goodness has already won over evil, so evil can NEVER win. Give each child a duplicated paper, personalised with his or her own name.

Don't be afraid, ...,
because I will look after you
and keep you safe.
You stick up for me
and I will stick up for you.
Together we'll make the world
a happier place.

They can decorate it and keep it to read whenever they need courage to do the right thing.

Things to Sing

Out to the great wide world (Wake up, World!)
God is making a wonderful world (Wake up, World!)
In the winter nights are dark (Wake up, World!)
I'm black, I'm white, I'm short, I'm tall (Wake up, World!)

New Beginnings with God

Things to Read

Isaiah 62:1-5
John 21:15-22
Revelation 3:14-end

Things to Do

Remind the children of how Peter had denied Jesus three times when he was frightened of what might happen to him if he told the truth. Discuss times when we feel scared of doing the right thing (like owning up, for instance) and how we don't feel really comfortable with someone we have hurt until we've said sorry and they have forgiven us.

Now tell or read how Jesus puts things right again for Peter, and even trusts him again. Jesus does the same with us – he will always give us another chance.

Help each child make a zig-zag picture to show how turning away from God makes him and us miserable. Turning back to him makes him and us happy. Each picture is coloured, cut in strips and pasted on to thin card in the order: 1A 2B 3C 4D etc. Fold the finished card like a fan, and the two pictures will emerge when viewed from one side or the other.

Things to Sing

God forgave my sin (*Songs and Hymns of Fellowship*)
Out to the great wide world we go (*Wake up, World!*)
Pick up your feet and go (*Wake up, World!*)
God is making a wonderful world (*Wake up, World!*)

1 2 3 4 5 6 7 8 9 10 11 12   A B C D E F G H I J K L

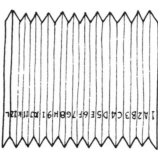

The Way, the Truth and the Life

Things to Read

Proverbs 4:10-19
2 Corinthians 4:13-5:5
John 14:1-11

Things to Do

Working on the theme of Jesus being 'The Way', begin by setting up two model villages, built by the children in lego or building blocks, in different parts of the room.

When they are finished, sit down with the children between the villages and talk about how the people could get from one to the other, through the wild countryside. They could have little arrows at intervals – but in fog you might get lost between the signs. They could have instructions, like: 'turn left at the second tree' – but suppose the wind blew a tree down, or another one grew up? You could lose your way.

What we really need is a clear road or track to walk along, which goes directly to the distant town. (Draw a road in chalk.) Now tell the children how Jesus said he was the Way, or road, to God in heaven, so if we want to get there we just have to follow him.

Help them make a spiritual map, with Baptism town at one corner, and The Heavenly City at another. The way winds round all kinds of dangerous mountains, rushing rivers, thick forests etc, but never disappears until it reaches the City. Along the road they write in: Jesus said, 'I am the Way'. Colour in the maps and display them in church if possible.

Things to Sing

One more step along the world I go *(Come and Praise)*
Keep on travelling on *(Wake up, World!)*
Pick up your feet and go *(Wake up, World!)*

God Makes Friends

Things to Read

Jeremiah 1:4-10
Mark 1:14-20
Acts 26:1, 9-20

Things to Do

As the children come in, make a point of having various jobs that need doing. In each case say something like: 'Now, we need someone strong to move this table'; 'We need two people to arrange these lovely flowers Matthew brought.' etc.

When everyone is ready, remind the children of these needs which various people offered to do. God also needs our help to do his work, and he is hoping we will offer our help so that he can use us to make the world a more loving, caring place. Lead the children in prayer –

Heavenly Father,
here I am –
please use me:
I would really like
to help you.

All of us here have been chosen and asked to help, just as the fishermen – Peter, Andrew, James and John – were chosen in Galilee. Tell or read today's gospel story.

Have a fishing net (or net curtain) and ask each child to make a fish, using templates for the younger children. They write their own names on the fish and decorate them. Then they poke the fish into the net so the names show. Hang the net up in church, putting a notice beside it saying: 'I will make you fishers of men'

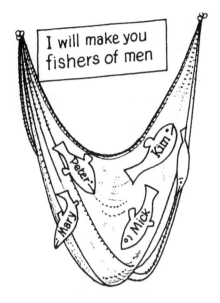

Things to Sing

Jesus had all kinds of friends *(Wake up, World!)*
He's got the whole world in his hand *(Come and praise)*
Put your hand in the hand

Being the People of God

Things to Read

2 Samuel 7:4-16
Luke 14:15-24
Acts 2:37-end

A children's version of the gospel story, as both a narrative and drama, entitled *Let's Have a Party!* can be found in *Wonderful World!* (Kevin Mayhew).

Things to Do

The gospel reading is good to use for making a 'television' programme. The television is a cereal packet with two wooden spoons for winding the 'film' on, and the story is displayed in a series of pictures on a long strip of paper, marked into numbered frames. Either the words can be written underneath each picture, or they can be read on to tape with a clicker between each frame so that the winder knows when to do his bit.

Tell the children the story first and have each part written on a separate card. These are then given out in order to the children, who work on a particular frame, either drawing or colouring in the appropriate picture. It may be easiest to work on the floor, or to stick separate sheets on to a strip when they are finished.

The finished story can be presented to others, perhaps during visits to the elderly, or those in hospital. It can be kept as useful resource material.

Things to Sing

Love is something, if you give it away
Come on and celebrate *(Songs and Hymns of Fellowship)*
Break the bread and pour the wine *(Wake up, World!)*
Out to the great wide world we go *(Wake up, World!)*

Be Like Jesus

Things to Read

Philippians 2:1-11
John 13:1-15

Things to Do

Have a display of all kinds of interesting and lovely things in God's world, and give the children some time to examine them, enjoy them and find out about them. (Have magnifying glasses handy, and direct their attention to colours, textures, behaviour etc.)

Talk together about the wonderful world, which shows us something about God, just as the pictures we paint show others something about us. Sing some praise songs, and then tell them how Jesus, in spite of all his greatness, acts like a servant. Explain how the servants of that time washed people's feet because it was a hot, dusty country. Then wash one or two children's feet to show them. What servant jobs can they do cheerfully, to follow Jesus' example? Arrange for them to help with clearing up the coffee cups after church, or doing some other very dull job in a happy, friendly way as an act of praise.

Things to Sing

Meekness and majesty
The servant king
God is making a wonderful world *(Wake up, World!)*
Out to the great wide world we go *(Wake up, World!)*

Our Mission to All People

Things to Read

Luke 10:1-12
Acts 11:4-18

Things to Do

Tell the children how Jesus sent out seventy-two people to go on ahead and prepare others for his coming. Choose some to be the disciples, and get them to take off their socks and shoes. Act out the rest of the gospel reading, with the other children being the people who are visited; some are ill and are cured, some make them welcome, and some don't. Show some pictures of Israel so the children can see that Jesus' instructions were practical for travelling light in that climate and terrain.

Gather round in prayer to ask Jesus to show us where he wants us to work for him today and through the week, and give them this prayer to colour and hang up in the bathroom at home and use every morning.

Things to Sing

God knows me *(Come and Praise)*
I'm black, I'm white, I'm short, I'm tall *(Wake up, World!)*
Out to the great wide world we go *(Wake up, World!)*

Father, I will give today to you
Show me how to spend it well

The Cost of Christian Living

Things to Read

Ezekiel 36:24-28
John 15:16-end
Galatians 5:16-25

Things to Do

Have ready two money boxes or piggy banks and some pretend money (or real, if you wish.) Read the first part of the gospel passage.

Explain how Jesus said that following him might be rather expensive, and we'd better decide first whether or not we're prepared to pay the cost before we join him.

What expenses are there in following Jesus? On another 'Christian Expenses' list, write down what we have to spend or give up to be Christians:

– watching television on Sunday mornings;
– telling lies;
– keeping all our sweets to ourselves;
– joining in the unkind teasing; etc.

What do we pay with? Out of the second money box take money shaped cards with:

– kindness;
– love;
– thoughtfulness;
– helpfulness;
– peace-making;
– self-control;
– patience;
– cheerfulness; etc.

It costs a lot, doesn't it? But we couldn't spend it on anything that would make us happier. And remind them that Jesus has spent everything for us – even his life!

Give each child a box to decorate and cut out 'coins' to put inside.

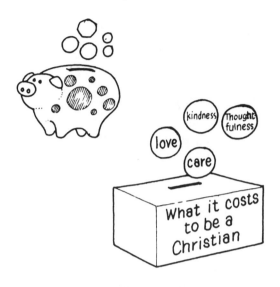

Things to Sing

Love is something if you give it away
Do this when you remember me (Wake up, World!)
Jesus had all kinds of friends (Wake up, World!)

Life-giving Spirit

Things to Read

Ezekiel 37:1-14
Luke 6:27-38
1 Corinthians 12:4-13

Things to Do

Read or tell the children the teachings in the gospel passage today, acting some of them out with different children as you go, and involving them in what they think is the right thing to do in each situation. They may well be surprised at Jesus' advice!

Then talk with them about the sort of thing they find starts them off behaving in an unloving way, and together work out some practical way to avoid the temptation. (Perhaps going out to kick a ball when they feel like kicking a sister; setting a cooking timer to share a toy equally, giving each a set time – until the pinger rings – in which to play; writing a list of daily jobs that need to be done before bed, so things don't get forgotten; asking to sit next to someone in class with whom they are less likely to waste time!)

Give the children paper cups and a pencil. They draw their own face on the side of the cup and punch holes in the bottom. Then, over the grass or a large bowl, pour water from an enormous jug through each child's cup. We are to be channels for God's living Spirit to flow through to the world; we have to work at increasing the flow!

Things to Sing

Peace is flowing like a river (You could add a verse: 'Life is flowing . . .') (Songs and Hymns of Fellowship)
Out to the great wide world we go (Wake up, World!)

Doing the Right Thing

Things to Read

1 Kings 3:4-15
Matthew 12:9-14
l Timothy 2:1-7

Things to Do

Prepare three large posters each with four sheets of paper stapled at the top, like this:

get done as well. The fourth circumstance helps the children explore the kind of situation when a good rule has to be broken in order to do God's will. Obeying God's law of love must always take precedence.

Next, deal with the question of Bible reading in the same way, and finally the question of prayer. This one will be different, because there is no time at all when keeping in touch with God is wrong; in fact, the more difficult the situation, the closer we cling!

After this discussion, show the children a picture of Jesus healing the man with the withered arm. Was it a good thing he was doing? Tell or read how the Pharisees reacted and how Jesus showed that even the best rules are not as important as living life in God's loving way.

Things to Sing

Love is something if you give it away
Put your hand in the hand
He was born in the winter in a draughty shed (*Wake up, World!*)

Look together at the one about going to church. The answer to the first two questions is going to be YES; the third circumstance is more difficult. In the end the answer should still be YES, as long as they plan to rearrange other activities that day to make sure the necessary jobs

Salt and Light

Things to Read

Micah 4:1-5
Matthew 5:13-16

Things to Do

Bring along the following:
– some sea salt;
– something preserved in brine (e.g. frankfurters);
– some small cubes of cheese (enough for one each)
– a candle;
– a large metal saucepan.

First sprinkle some grains of salt on a plate and talk about what it is (they can taste it if they like). Explain how it was used to keep food before anyone had freezers and fridges. Sometimes it is still used like that (give examples) and in hotter countries it is still used to preserve meat and fish. See if they can taste the saltiness in cheese – the salt keeps it fresh.

Now read what Jesus said about us being salt. Discuss with them what this means for us: how can we be salt in the world? It may be helpful to have this question on a board or sheet of paper, and jot down their ideas to keep track of them.

Then light the candle, and talk about useful lights such as torches, street lamps, car lights etc. Cover the light with the saucepan, and help them see how silly this is, if we want to light the room.

Now read the second part of today's gospel passage and jot down ideas under a second question: how can we be the light of the world?

Help the children to make these Chinese lanterns from stiff paper. They can carry them into church.

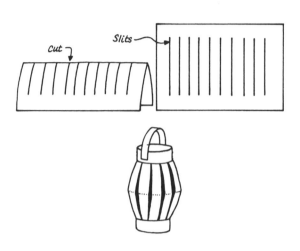

Things to Sing

I'm gonna let my little light shine
Out to the great wide world we go (*Wake up, World!*)
God is making a wonderful world (*Wake up, World!*)

Generous Giving

Things to Read

1 Chronicles 29:1-9
Matthew 20:1-16
Philippians 1:1-11

A children's version of the gospel story, both as narrative and as drama, entitled *Everyone Gets the Same* is available in *Wonderful World!* (Kevin Mayhew).

Things to Do

First discuss with the children what work there is in a vineyard, such as grape picking, treading the grapes, weeding, pruning etc. Everyone can act out each job.

Without telling the story first, begin acting it out, with one child taking the part of the landowner. Narrate it simply, and split the other children into five groups (or fewer if numbers are small) to be the workers hanging around the market place. Make sure that the first group is quite clear about how much money they will earn – let them shake hands during the deal. And make much of those who work hard during the hot blistering day.

When it comes to the giving out of wages, see how the children react to the amount the last workers are given, but don't give away the surprise. When the first workers receive their wages it will be interesting to see how they take it, and it should give rise to some lively discussion on what is fair and what is generous.

Bring out two points:

1. Jesus never gives up looking for us in the market place to see if we'd like to work for him.

2. If we do decide to give him our time and energy, then even if we were a long while getting there, Jesus will welcome us and we shall not lose the good reward at the end.

Help the children make a model of a vineyard and workers out of plasticine, and assorted boxes, paper, string, pipecleaners etc.

Things to Sing

Come on and celebrate *(Songs and Hymns of Fellowship)*
God is making a wonderful world *(Wake up, World!)*
Love is something if you give it away

Loving Service

Things to Read

Isaiah 42:1-7
John 13:31-35
2 Corinthians 4:1-10

Things to Do

Collect some pictures of missionary work, both at home and abroad, and discuss with the children what the needs are and how they are being met. Point out that the missionaries are telling people about the God of love not only by what they say but also how they behave and what they do.

Discuss with them the kind of things they would like others to know about their special friend, Jesus – who he was, how he helps them and what he is like.

Write down their words on coloured paper which they can illustrate, and then staple the whole lot together to make a book. If possible have it duplicated and used as an aid in mission; children's straightforward and trusting faith is a great witness.

Things to Sing

When I needed a neighbour *(Come and Praise)*
Love is something if you give it away
Out to the great wide world we go *(Wake up, World!)*
Come on and celebrate *(Songs and Hymns of Fellowship)*

The Best Offering

Things to Read

Deuteronomy 26:1-11
Matthew 5:17-26
2 Corinthians 8:1-9

Things to Do

Tell the children (or remind them) of how God had helped the people escape from Egypt where they had been slaves, and how, when they reached the promised land, they thanked God every year by bringing a basket of their harvest to his altar. At our harvest festival we do the same. If we remember that God is the provider of all we have, our lives will be rich and full; God holds everything together. Spread out the five sections of this jigsaw puzzle and ask two of the children to make the puzzle up.

If we have God at the centre, all the different parts of our lives can be part of our thanks and praise. Give out pieces of thin card, paper with the puzzle drawn on, scissors, glue and crayons, and help them make their own jigsaws to take home.

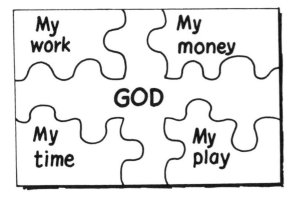

Things to Sing

Come on and celebrate *(Songs and Hymns of Fellowship)*
The best gift
Love is something if you give it away
God is making a wonderful world *(Wake up, World!)*
You shall go out with joy *(Songs and Hymns of Fellowship)*

Using God's Gifts

Things to Read

Nehemiah 6:1-16
Matthew 25:14-30
1 Peter 4:7-11

A children's version of the gospel story, as both narrative and drama, entitled *What Have You Done With My Money?*, can be found in *Wonderful World!* (Kevin Mayhew).

Things to Do

Have three boxes with slits in the lids, and some play money. Label the boxes as follows:

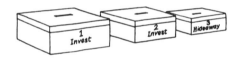

Secretly place five pounds inside box 1, two pounds inside box 2 and nothing in box 3.

Tell the children the story of today's Gospel, using more play money. Post five pounds into the first box, two pounds into the second box and one pound into the third.

When you tell the children about the master's return, open each lid. There will now be ten pounds in the first (give him a round of applause), four pounds in the second (another round of applause), and still only one in the last.

Explain how Jesus needs us to use the gifts he gives us, otherwise they will be wasted. Talk with them about their own gifts and things they are good at or advantages they have been given. These may include, for instance, being friendly, strong, a fast runner, musical, clever, artistic, sympathetic, good with animals, a clear reader, funny, or a good listener. They may also include having enough money to share, outgrown toys which could be given away, or time which might be used in helping.

Things to Sing

God is making a wonderful world *(Wake up, World!)*
Love is something if you give it away

God's Law of Love

Things to Read

Exodus 20:1-17
Matthew 19:16-26
Ephesians 5:1-10

Things to Do

Have plenty of Bibles available and help the children to find the verses in which the ten commandments are written. It is important that the children are familiar with these and how Moses received them from God. Older children can be encouraged to learn them, with a small prize given to all who manage to do so.

Talk with the children about good manners, and rules they have at home and at school. These are written up on a board or sheet entitled: 'Remember your manners!' They may include:

Keep to the left in the corridor.
Don't speak with your mouth full.
Please and thank you.
Say 'hallo' and 'goodbye'.
Don't interrupt.
Offer food.
Turn T.V. off if visitor comes.
Open classroom door to teacher.
Stand at side for people to pass.
Wait your turn in a queue.

Point out that these are ways of caring for others and respecting them. If you love someone, you do this anyway. The rules remind you to act lovingly however you feel about the other person.

Have a lot of supermarket cartons, with the biggest labelled 'Love God with all your heart and soul and mind and strength'. Label the others: 'Friends', 'Money', 'Career', 'Home', 'Holidays', 'Car' etc. Then place the commandments box in the centre of the room and ask the children to help build their lives on it, to make a tall tower. What happens if we take away our base of loving God? Have a volunteer to pull out that main box and watch all the rest come tumbling down.

Things to Sing

When I needed a neighbour *(Come and Praise)*
Lord of the dance
Love is something if you give it away
I'm black, I'm white, I'm short, I'm tall *(Wake up, World!)*

THINGS TO DO

Index of Uses

CHRISTIAN THEMES

Faith, Trust, Hope
Children of God
Choosing God's Way
Get Ready for God
God Forgives and Heals
God is Shown to the World
God Offers Us New Life
God of Surprises
God Saves and Judges
God Saves his People
Good News for Mary
Good will Overcome Evil
Hear God Calling
How Faith Grows
Individuals Matter to God
Jesus is Alive!
Jesus is Coming
Jesus Suffered for Us
Let the Light Shine
Listen to God!
Look Out for God
New Beginnings with God
One Great Family
Prepare the Way!
Ready and Waiting
Saved by Christ
Sharing Jesus' Baptism
Sign of God's Glory
The Good Shepherd
The Light of God's Glory
The Prophets Point to Jesus
Who is Jesus?

Sin, Repentance, Forgiveness
Children of God and Friends of Jesus
Churches, Temples and People
God Changes Lives
God Forgives and Heals
Good will Overcome Evil
Individuals Matter to God
Jesus Suffered for Us
New Beginnings with God
Prepare the Way!
Room For Us All!
Sharing Jesus' Baptism

Grace
Children of God
Children of God and Friends of Jesus

Faith and Prayer
Faith Without Seeing
Generous Giving
God Changes Lives
God is Wise
God Makes Friends
God Offers Us New Life
God's Mysterious Spirit
Good News for Mary
How Faith Grows
Individuals Matter to God
Jesus is Born
Jesus is Coming
Jesus Suffered for Us
Jesus Wipes Away Sins
Let the Light Shine
Life-giving Spirit
One Great Family
Our God Reigns
Room For Us All!
Sharing Jesus' Baptism
Sign of God's Glory
The Good Shepherd
The Hope of Heaven
The Light of God's Glory

Healing
Doing the Right thing
God Forgives and Heals
God Offers Us New Life
Healing and Wholeness
I Can See!
Room For Us All!
Saved by Christ
The Prophets Point to Jesus
Who is Jesus?

Jesus, Saviour and King
Faith and Prayer
Faith Without Seeing
God is Shown to the World
God is Wise
God of Surprises
God Saves and Judges
God's Way is Different – and Better!
God Turns Sorrow into Joy
Good News for Mary
Good will Overcome Evil
Individuals Matter to God
Jesus is Alive!
Jesus is Born

Jesus is Coming
Jesus Suffered for Us
Let the Light Shine
New Beginnings with God
Our God Reigns
Prepare the Way!
Room For Us All!
Saved by Christ
Sign of God's Glory
Taking Responsibility
The Bible Shows us Jesus
The Cost of Love and Forgiveness
The Good Shepherd
The Hope of Heaven
The King on a Donkey
The Light of God's Glory
The Light of the World
The Prophets Point to Jesus
The Way, the Truth and the Life
Who is Jesus?

Prayer
Faith and Prayer
Falling Away from Goodness
Generous Giving
Healing and Wholeness
Hear God Calling
Honest Worship
Hope and Pray
Keeping Hope Alive
Listen to God!
Ready and Waiting

THE CHURCH: THE PEOPLE OF GOD

Serving
Be Like Jesus
Choosing God's Way
Courage and Commitment
Faith and Works
Generous Giving
God Makes Friends
God's Way is Different – and Better!
Good Neighbours
Good News for Mary
Hope and Pray
Life-giving Spirit
Listen to God!
Love in Action

Loving Service
New Beginnings with God
Offering and Sharing
Salt and Light
The Best Offering
The Cost of Christian Living
The Good Shepherd
The King on a Donkey
The Prophets Point to Jesus
Using God's Gifts
Who is Jesus?

Witnessing

Courage and Commitment
Faith and Works
Faith Without Seeing
God Changes Lives
God is Shown to the World
God is Wise
God's Mysterious Spirit
God's Way is Different – and Better!
Good News for Mary
Hear God Calling
Individuals Matter to God
Jesus is Alive!
Jesus is Born
Let the Light Shine
Living by Faith
Loving Service
Our Mission to All People
Prepare the Way!
Room For Us All!
Salt and Light
The Bible Shows us Jesus
The Cost of Love and Forgiveness
The Good Shepherd
The Hope of Heaven
The Light of God's Glory
The Light of the World
The Prophets Point to Jesus
Who is Jesus?

Suffering

Courage and Commitment
Faith Without Seeing
God Offers Us New Life
God Turns Sorrow into Joy
Good will Overcome Evil
Healing and Wholeness
Jesus Suffered for Us
Let the Light Shine
Ready and Waiting
Sharing Jesus' Baptism
Taking Responsibility
The Cost of Love and Forgiveness
The Good Shepherd
The King on a Donkey

Watching and Waiting

Get Ready for God
God of Surprises

God's Mysterious Spirit
God Saves and Judges
Good News for Mary
How Faith Grows
Jesus is Alive!
Jesus is Coming
Look Out for God
Our God Reigns
Prepare the Way!
Ready and Waiting
The Cost of Love and Forgiveness

The Journey of Life

Abraham's Faith
God is Shown to the World
God Saves his People
God Turns Sorrow into Joy
Jesus is Coming
Keeping Hope Alive
Listen to God!
Our Mission to All People
The Light of the World
The Way, the Truth and the Life

The Family

Children of God
Children of God and Friends of Jesus
Jesus is Born
One Great Family

Church Unity

Children of God
Children of God and Friends of Jesus
Churches, Temples and People
Faith and Works
Falling Away from Goodness
Forgiveness
God's Mysterious Spirit
Life-giving Spirit
Loving and Forgiving
Offering and Sharing
One Great Family
Room For Us All!
Seventy Times Seven
The Bible Shows us Jesus
The Good Shepherd
The Hope of Heaven

WORSHIP

The Ministry of the Word

Individuals Matter to God
Prepare the Way!
The Bible Shows us Jesus
The Prophets Point to Jesus

Holy Communion

Be Like Jesus
Being the People of God
Children of God

God Turns Sorrow into Joy
Jesus the Bread of Life
Love in Action
New Beginnings with God
Offering and Sharing
Sign of God's Glory

Baptism/Church Membership

Being the People of God
Children of God
Children of God and Friends of Jesus
God Makes Friends
God's Mysterious Spirit
God Offers Us New Life
Individuals Matter to God
Life-giving Spirit
Loving and Forgiving
New Beginnings with God
Our Mission to All People
Saved by Christ
Sharing Jesus' Baptism
Stand Firm
The King on a Donkey
The Way, the Truth and the Life

Ecumenical Worship

See Church Unity

THE CHURCH'S YEAR

Advent

Children of God
Get Ready for God
God of Surprises
God Saves and Judges
Good News for Mary
Good will Overcome Evil
Jesus is Coming
Look Out for God
New Beginnings with God
Prepare the Way!
The Prophets Point to Jesus
Who is Jesus?

Christmas/Epiphany

Children of God
God is Shown to the World
Jesus is Born
The Light of the World

Lent

Churches, Temples and People
God's Way is Different – and Better!
Honest Worship
Individuals Matter to God
Jesus Suffered for Us
Keeping Hope Alive
Let the Light Shine
Love in Action
Ready and Waiting

Seventy Times Seven
Sharing Jesus' Baptism
Stand Firm
The King on a Donkey
The Light of God's Glory

Maundy Thursday
Be Like Jesus

Good Friday
The Cost of Love and Forgiveness

Easter
Faith Without Seeing
God Offers Us New Life
God Turns Sorrow into Joy
Jesus is Alive!
New Beginnings with God
Room For Us All!
Saved by Christ

Ascension
Our God Reigns
The Hope of Heaven

Pentecost
God's Mysterious Spirit
Life-giving Spirit

Harvest
Jesus the Bread of Life
God Made the Earth
Good Neighbours
How Faith Grows
Love in Action
Offering and Sharing
Our Mission to All People
Room For Us All!
The Best Offering
Wonderful World!

INDEX OF BIBLICAL CHARACTERS

Abraham
Abraham's Faith
Living by Faith
Love in Action

Adam/Adam and Eve
Wonderful World!
Taking Responsibility

Agrippa
God Makes Friends

Andrew
God Makes Friends
Hear God Calling

Annas
The Cost of Love and Forgiveness

Barabbas
The Cost of Love and Forgiveness

Blind Bartimaeus
I Can See!

Caiaphas
The Cost of Love and Forgiveness

Cain and Abel
Falling Away From Goodness

Children
One Great Family

Cleopas
God Turns Sorrow into Joy

David
Forgiveness
Generous Giving

Daniel
God Changes Lives

David
Being the People of God

Eli
Hear God Calling

Elijah
God of Surprises
Let the Light Shine
The Light of God's Glory
The Hope of Heaven

Elishah
Healing and Wholeness
The Hope of Heaven

Ethiopian Eunuch
Individuals Matter to God

Gabriel
Good News for Mary

'Good' Samaritan
Good Neighbours

Herod
God is Shown to the World
The Light of the World
Who is Jesus?

Jacob
Living by Faith

James and John
God Makes Friends
Let the Light Shine
The Light of God's Glory

Jairus's Daughter
Saved by Christ

Jesus
Abraham's Faith
Be Like Jesus
Children of God
Churches, Temples and People
Doing the Right Thing
Faith Without Seeing
God Changes Lives
God is Wise
God Made the Earth
God Makes Friends
God Turns Sorrow into Joy
Good News for Mary
Healing and Wholeness
Hear God Calling
I Can See!
Jesus is Born
Jesus is Coming
Jesus the Bread of Life
Jesus Wipes Away Sins
Let the Light Shine
New Beginnings with God
Offering and Sharing
One Great Family
Our God Reigns
Room For Us All!
Saved by Christ
Sharing Jesus' Baptism
Sign of God's Glory
The Bible Shows us Jesus
The Cost of Love and Forgiveness
The Hope of Heaven
The King on a Donkey
The Light of God's Glory
The Light of the World
The Way, the Truth and the Life
Who is Jesus?
Wonderful World!

John the Baptist
God Made the Earth
Hear God Calling
Prepare the Way!
Sharing Jesus' Baptism
The Light of God's Glory
Who is Jesus?

Joshua
Keeping Hope Alive

Judas Iscariot
The Cost of Love and Forgiveness

Lazarus and the Rich Man
Love in Action

Malchus
The Cost of Love and Forgiveness

Man with a withered hand
Doing the Right Thing

Mary (and Joseph)
Good News for Mary
Jesus is Born
Jesus is Coming
Sign of God's Glory
The Cost of Love and Forgiveness
The Light of the World

Mary Magdalene
Jesus is Alive!
The Cost of Love and Forgiveness

Moses
God's Mysterious Spirit
God Saves his People
Individuals Matter to God
Keeping Hope Alive
Let the Light Shine
The Light of God's Glory

Naaman
Healing and Wholeness

Nathan
Being the People of God

Nathanael
Hear God Calling

Nebuchadnezzar
Courage and Commitment

Nicodemus
Wonderful World!

Noah
Listen to God!

Paul
God Makes Friends
Hope and Pray

Peter
Be Like Jesus
God Makes Friends
Hear God Calling
Let the Light Shine
New Beginnings with God
Our Mission to All people
Room For Us All!
The Cost of Love and Forgiveness
The Light of God's Glory

Philip
Hear God Calling
Individuals Matter to God
The Way, the Truth and the Life

Pilate
The Cost of Love and Forgiveness

Priests, Scribes and Pharisees
God Forgives and Heals
God is Wise
Good Neighbours
Jesus Wipes Away Sins
One Great Family
Prepare the Way!
The Cost of Love and Forgiveness

Prodigal Son
Loving and Forgiving

Samuel
Hear God Calling

Saul (King)
Forgiveness

Simon the Pharisee
Forgiveness

Shadrach, Meschah and Abednego
Courage and Commitment

Shepherds
Jesus is Born

Solomon
Churches, Temples and People
Doing the Right Thing
Generous Giving

Sower
How Faith Grows

Syro-Phenician Woman
Healing and Wholeness

Thomas
Faith Without Seeing
The Way, the Truth and the Life

Unjust Judge
Hope and Pray

Unjust Steward
Choosing God's Way

Wise and Foolish Bridesmaids
Look Out for God

Wise Men
God is Shown to the World
The Light of the World

Woman Caught in Adultery
Jesus Wipes Away Sins

Woman with Ointment
Forgiveness

INDEX OF BIBLICAL REFERENCES

Genesis 1:1-31
God Made the Earth

Genesis 2:4b-9
Wonderful World!

Genesis 2:7-9; 3:1-7
Taking Responsibility

Genesis 4:1-16
Falling Away From Goodness

Genesis 6:11-end
Listen to God!

Genesis 12:1-9
Abraham's Faith

Genesis 28:10-end
Living by Faith

Exodus 3:1-6
The Light of God's Glory

Exodus 6:2-8
God Saves his People

Exodus 19:16-25
God's Mysterious Spirit

Exodus 20:1-17
God's Law of Love

Exodus 33:12-end
Sign of God's Glory

Exodus 34:29-end
Let the Light Shine

Leviticus 19:9-end
Good Neighbours

Deuteronomy 6:17-end
God Offers Us New Life

Deuteronomy 7:6-11
Children of God and Friends of Jesus

Deuteronomy 8:1-6
Offering and Sharing

Deuteronomy 11 :18-28
Choosing God's Way

Deuteronomy 15:7-11
Love in Action

Deuteronomy 26:1-11
The Best Offering

Deuteronomy 34
Keeping Hope Alive

93

1 Samuel 3:1-10
Hear God Calling

1 Samuel 24:1-17
Forgiveness

2 Samuel 7:4-16
Being the People of God

1 Kings 3:4-15
Doing the Right thing

1 Kings 8:22-30
Churches, Temples and People

1 Kings 19:9-18
God of Surprises

2 Kings 2:1-15
The Hope of Heaven

2 Kings 5:1-14
Healing and Wholeness

1 Chronicles 29:1-9
Generous Giving

Nehemiah 6:1-16
Using God's Gifts

Proverbs 2:1-9
God is Wise

Proverbs 3:1-8
How Faith Grows

Proverbs 4:10-19
The Way, the Truth and the Life

Isaiah 7:10-14
Children of God

Isaiah 9:2-7
Jesus is Born

Isaiah 11:1-9
Good News for Mary

Isaiah 12
Jesus is Alive!

Isaiah 25:6-9
God Turns Sorrow into Joy

Isaiah 33:17-22
Look Out for God

Isaiah 40:1-11
Prepare the Way!

Isaiah 42:1-7
Loving Service
Sharing Jesus' Baptism

Isaiah 43:16-21
Jesus is Alive!

Isaiah 49:1-6
God is Shown to the World

Isaiah 50:4-9
Jesus Suffered for Us

Isaiah 51:4-11
God Saves and Judges

Isaiah 52:7-10
Get Ready for God

Isaiah 52:13-53:12
The Cost of Love and Forgiveness

Isaiah 53:5
Jesus Suffered for Us

Isaiah 55:1-11
The Bible Shows us Jesus

Isaiah 60:1-6
Jesus Suffered for Us
The Light of the World

Isaiah 61:1-7
Room For Us All!

Isaiah 62:1-5
New Beginnings with God

Isaiah 63:7-14
Individuals Matter to God

Isaiah 64:1-7
The Prophets Point to Jesus

Jeremiah 1:4-10
God Makes Friends

Jeremiah 7:1-11
Honest Worship

Ezekiel 34:7-16
The Good Shepherd

Ezekiel 36:24-28
The Cost of Christian Living

Ezekiel 37:1-14
Life-giving Spirit

Daniel 3:13-26
Courage and Commitment

Daniel 6:10-22
God Changes Lives

Daniel 7:9-14
Jesus Suffered for Us
Our God Reigns

Hosea 6:1-6
Good will Overcome Evil

Hosea 11:1-9
Seventy Times Seven

Micah 4:1-5
Salt and Light

Micah 5:2
Jesus Suffered for Us

Zephaniah 3:14-end
God Forgives and Heals

Habakkuk 2:1-4
Hope and Pray

Malachi 3:1-5
Who is Jesus?

Matthew 1:18-23
Jesus is Coming

Matthew 2:1-12, 19-23
God is Shown to the World
The Light of the World

Matthew 3:13-end
Sharing Jesus' Baptism

Matthew 4:1-11
Taking Responsibility

Matthew 5:1-12
God's Way is Different – and Better!

Matthew 5:13-16
Salt and Light

Matthew 5:17-26
The Best Offering

Matthew 6:24-end
Living by Faith

Matthew 7:13-27
Stand Firm

Matthew 11:2-15
Who is Jesus?

Matthew 12:9-14
Doing the Right thing

Matthew 12:38-42
God is Wise

Matthew 17:1-13
The Light of God's Glory

Matthew 18:21-end
Seventy Times Seven

Matthew 19:16-26
God's Law of Love

Matthew 20:1-16
Generous Giving

Matthew 21:1-9
The King on a Donkey

Matthew 24:37-44
God of Surprises

Matthew 25:1-13
Look Out For God

Matthew 25:14-30
Using God's Gifts

Matthew 25:31-46
God Saves and Judges

Matthew 28:1-10
Jesus is Alive!

Mark 1:7-11
The Bible Shows us Jesus

Mark 1:14-20
God Makes Friends

Mark 2:1-12
God Forgives and Heals

Mark 7:14-23
Falling Away from Goodness

Mark 7:24-end
Healing and Wholeness

Mark 10:2-16
One Great Family

Mark 10:46-end
I Can See!

Mark 13:5-13
God Saves his People

Mark 13:14-23
Ready and Waiting

Luke 1:26-38
Good News for Mary

Luke 2:1-20
Jesus is Born

Luke 4:14-21
The Prophets Point to Jesus

Luke 6:27-38
Life-giving Spirit

Luke 7:36-end
Forgiveness

Luke 8:4-15
How Faith Grows

Luke 8:41-end
Saved by Christ

Luke 9:28-36
Let the Light Shine

Luke 9:51-end
Courage and Commitment

Luke 10:1-12
Our Mission to All People

Luke 10:25-37
Good Neighbours

Luke 11:1-13
Faith and Prayer

Luke 14:15-24
Being the People of God

Luke 15:1-10
Individuals Matter to God

Luke 15:11-end
Loving and Forgiving

Luke 16:1-9
Choosing God's Way

Luke 16:19-end
Love in Action

Luke 18:1-8
Hope and Pray

Luke 19:1-10
God Changes Lives

Luke 20:9-17
Faith and Works

Luke 21:25-33
Get Ready for God

Luke 24:13-35
God Turns Sorrow into Joy

Luke 24:45-end
Our God Reigns
The Hope of Heaven

John 1:1-14
God Made the Earth

John 1:14-18
Children of God

John 1:19-28
Prepare the Way!

John 1:35-end
Hear God Calling

John 2:1-11
Sign of God's Glory

John 2:13-22
Churches, Temples and People

John 3:1-8
Wonderful World!

John 4:19-26
Honest Worship

John 5:36-end
The Bible Shows us Jesus

John 6:1-14
Offering and Sharing

John 6:5-14, 35
Jesus the Bread of Life

John 8:2-11
Jesus Wipes Away Sins

John 8:51-end
Abraham's Faith

John 10:7-16
The Good Shepherd

John 13:31-35
Loving Service

John 13:1-15
Be Like Jesus

John 14:1-11
The Way, the Truth and the Life

John 14:15-26
God's Mysterious Spirit

John 15:5-11
God Offers Us New Life

John 15:12-17
Children of God and Friends of Jesus

John 15:16-end
The Cost of Christian Living

John 16:1-11
Jesus Suffered for Us

John 16:12-24
Keeping Hope Alive

John 16:25-end
Good will Overcome Evil

John 18:1-19:37
The Cost of Love and Forgiveness

John 20:19-29
Faith Without Seeing

John 21:1-14
Room For Us All!

John 21:15-22
New Beginnings with God

Acts 2:1-21
God's Mysterious Spirit

Acts 2:37-end
Being the People of God

Acts 4:8-12
Saved by Christ

Acts 8:26-38
Individuals Matter to God

Acts 11:4-18
Our Mission to All people

Acts 26:1-8
Hope and Pray

Acts 26:1, 9-20
God Makes Friends

Romans 4:13-end
Abraham's Faith

Romans 6:3-11
God Offers Us New Life

Romans 8:18-25
Courage and Commitment

Romans 8:35-end
Keeping Hope Alive

Romans 9:19-28
Ready and Waiting

Romans 12:9-end
Good Neighbours

Romans 13:8-end
God Saves and Judges

Romans 15:4-13
The Prophets Point to Jesus

1 Corinthians 1:26-end
Good News for Mary

1 Corinthians 3:10-17
Churches, Temples and People

1 Corinthians 3:18-end
God is Wise

1 Corinthians 4:8-13
God's Way is Different – and Better!

1 Corinthians 12:4-13
Life-giving Spirit

1 Corinthians 13
Seventy Times Seven

1 Corinthians 15:1-11
Room For Us All!

1 Corinthians 15:21-28
Good Will Overcome Evil

2 Corinthians 4:1-10
Loving Service

2 Corinthians 4:13-5:5
The Way, the Truth and the Life

2 Corinthians 8:1-9
The Best Offering

2 Corinthians 12:1-10
Healing and Wholeness

Galatians 1:11-end
Hear God Calling

Galatians 3:23-4:7
Children of God and Friends of Jesus

Galatians 4:1-7
Children of God

Galatians 5:16-25
The Cost of Christian Living

Galatians 6:1-10
Forgiveness

Ephesians 1:15-end
Our God Reigns

Ephesians 2:1-10
Sharing Jesus' Baptism

Ephesians 3:1-12
God is Shown to the World

Ephesians 3:14-end
Faith and Prayer

Ephesians 4:1-13
The Hope of Heaven

Ephesians 4:17-end
I Can See!

Ephesians 5:1-10
God's Law of Love

Ephesians 5:25-6:4
One Great Family

Philippians 1:1-11
Generous Giving

Philippians 2:1-11
Be Like Jesus
The King on a Donkey

Philippians 4:10-20
Offering and Sharing

Colossians 1:18-23
Jesus Wipes Away Sins

Colossians 3:12-17
Loving and Forgiving

1 Thessalonians 5:1-11
Get Ready for God

1 Timothy 2:1-7
Doing the Right thing

2 Timothy 3:14-4:5
The Bible Shows us Jesus

Hebrews 2:14-end
Taking Responsibility

Hebrews 11:1-2, 8-16
Living by Faith

Hebrews 12:18-end
Honest Worship

James 2:14-26
Faith and Works

1 Peter 1:3-9
Faith Without Seeing

1 Peter 2:4-7
Stand Firm

1 Peter 4:7-11
Using God's Gifts

1 Peter 5:1-11
The Good Shepherd

2 Peter 1:16-19
The Light of God's Glory

1 John 3:9-18
Falling Away From Goodness

1 John 4:15-end
Love in Action

Revelation 3:14-end
New Beginnings with God

Revelation 4
Wonderful World!

Revelation 21:1-7
Jesus is Coming